Aristocracy: A Very Short Introduction

Very Short Introductions available now:

Available soon:

For more information visit our web site

www.oup.co.uk/general/vsi/

William Doyle

ARISTOCRACY

A Very Short Introduction

OXFORD
UNIVERSITY PRESS

OXFORD
UNIVERSITY PRESS

Great Clarendon Street, Oxford OX2 6DP

Oxford University Press is a department of the University of Oxford.
It furthers the University's objective of excellence in research, scholarship,
and education by publishing worldwide in

Oxford New York

Auckland Cape Town Dar es Salaam Hong Kong Karachi
Kuala Lumpur Madrid Melbourne Mexico City Nairobi
New Delhi Shanghai Taipei Toronto

With offices in

Argentina Austria Brazil Chile Czech Republic France Greece
Guatemala Hungary Italy Japan Poland Portugal Singapore
South Korea Switzerland Thailand Turkey Ukraine Vietnam

Oxford is a registered trade mark of Oxford University Press
in the UK and in certain other countries

Published in the United States
by Oxford University Press Inc., New York

British Library Cataloguing in Publication Data
Data available

Library of Congress Cataloging in Publication Data
Data available

Typeset by SPI Publisher Services, Pondicherry, India
Printed in Great Britain by
Ashford Colour Press Ltd, Gosport, Hampshire

ISBN 978-0-19-920678-0

1 3 5 7 9 10 8 6 4 2

In memory of Derek Waters, a natural gentleman

Contents

List of illustrations

Introduction

We use the words *aristocracy* and *aristocratic* all the time. We tend to apply them to groups, institutions, or behaviour which we see as exclusive, superior, proud, and more often than not, rich. Not infrequently, there is even an element of admiration. These connotations derive from long-standing claims made by the social elites who dominated European societies and systems of power from ancient times until relatively recently. In Europe, their relics are all around us. We instinctively recognize, sometimes even treasure, them, although we no longer accord them the unquestioning deference which those they evoke could once command.

These relics were usually designed to impress. They still do, although the target audience of underlings has long dissolved. Their confident façades, however, often conceal as much as they proclaim. Aristocratic hegemony has often been more precarious and less self-assured than it liked to appear. Aristocratic behaviour has been a good deal less pure and unsullied than the lofty principles supposedly guiding it. The history of aristocracies, in fact, is littered with self-serving myths which outsiders have been surprisingly willing to accept uncritically. The results of recent generations of historical research and scholarship leave little excuse for continuing to do so. This little book, based upon many years of teaching and writing about aristocrats and their ways, attempts to incorporate those results into a more detached survey of how they organized themselves, exercised authority, and eventually lost it.

The first chapter traces the history and evolution of the term, and attempts to offer the elements of an objective definition. It is followed by a chapter surveying the more subjective views of aristocrats themselves. Norms of aristocratic behaviour are the subject of the third chapter, while the fourth examines some of the ways in which aristocrats, their values, and their behaviour have influenced the rest of society beyond their ranks. The most important thing about aristocracies, from a 21st-century perspective, is that they and their influence have largely disappeared. How this came about, when over the centuries they have met and overcome so many other challenges, is the subject of the final chapter.

Chapter 1
Meanings and entitlements

Aristocracy is a word coined in ancient Greece. Originally it
meant not a group of people but a form of government: rule by
the best. But who were they?

From constitution to class

Plato thought (in the *Republic*) that the best people would be those
most expert at identifying and pursuing the common interest.
They would be called 'guardians', professional rulers and leaders.
As such, they would receive a long and careful training, and
enjoy no substantial property that might induce them to pursue
private interest rather than public. Much of this was implicit
criticism of the way city-states were actually governed in
Plato's time. But Plato's republic was not thought practical by
his most distinguished pupil; Aristotle preferred description to
prescription, and he offered a definition of aristocracy based upon
observation. It was a form of government 'in which more than one,
but not many, rule . . . and it is so called, either because the rulers
are the best men, or because they have at heart the best interests of
the state and its citizens'. It was thus the rule of a virtuous few; but
was easily perverted into mere oligarchy 'when it has in view the
interests only of the wealthy'. In an extreme oligarchy, the
governing class 'keep offices in their own hands, and the law
ordains that the son shall succeed the father'. But Aristotle was

realistic: wealth was essential to underpin the leisure and lack of temptation necessary for holders of public office, and so in aristocracies magistrates were chosen 'both according to their wealth and according to their merit'. And if 'the principle of an aristocracy is virtue', this quality was more likely to be found among people of 'birth and education', good birth being 'only ancient wealth and virtue'.

The aristocratic form of government therefore had distinct social overtones from its earliest formulation. Good birth had been a prized distinction in Greece for centuries before Plato and Aristotle. For the oldest classical poets, Hesiod and Homer, heroes exulted in descent from figures of legend, not to say gods. In ancient Rome, too, distinguished ancestry brought prestige, privilege, and entitlements to power. Along with the Greek word 'aristocracy', the terms used by the Romans to denote hereditary distinction would echo down the whole history of European government and social organization. The social elite of the early republic were the presumed descendants of the city's founding fathers, known as patricians. Exclusive and impenetrable, even so the patrician order never enjoyed unfettered dominance. It was inexorably compelled, down the republican centuries, to open public office and power to outsiders. Rich ones emerged over time as a secondary elite, the equestrians. So called after notional origins as mounted warriors, they were non-patricians rich enough to possess those expensive items, horses. And after epic struggles in the 4th and 3rd centuries BC, ordinary citizens, the plebeians, also achieved political equality. As a result, office-holding, and descent from office-holders, became the pre-eminent distinction. Families known for such a lineage, irrespective of their extraction, called themselves 'noble' (*nobiles*: 'known' and 'noble' having the same root). They kept masks of their illustrious ancestors in their houses, and engaged actors to impersonate them on public occasions. With few exceptions, consuls (the two magistrates elected annually to lead the republic) were from noble families. And when their terms were over, consuls entered the Senate, the republic's highest

1. A Roman nobleman with his ancestors

deliberative body which supposedly brought together the collective wisdom of all citizens with experience of high office. Membership of the Senate never exceeded a thousand, and for most of its history it was much smaller. This made senatorial families the most exclusive Roman elite of all. But more loosely, patricians, equestrians, nobles, and senators saw themselves as simply the best people (*optimates*). Cicero, an equestrian senator steeped in Greek thought and familiar with Aristotle, spent much of his career during the 1st century BC trying to rally the best people to their duty against a democratic and demagogic tide, the power of the so-called popular party (*populares*). He failed, but after the civil wars which cost Cicero his life, Augustus and his imperial successors recognized the traditional elites and their claims to distinction. If nobility and the display of its attributes slowly died out over the imperial centuries, patrician and equestrian identities, and above all, a senatorial order, remained at the summit of Roman society until its downfall. Roman precedents, and Roman models, would dominate most later theoretical discussions of what nobility meant and how nobles ought to behave.

By late antiquity, however, the hallowed names derived from republican times were applied to groups and institutions bearing only remote resemblance to their distant prototypes. They were all now embraced in a general category of 'more respectable people' (*honestiores*), and later emperors introduced subdivisions and differential titles of prestige. These proved a precedent, too, but only two late Roman titles found a place in subsequent titular hierarchies. Early in the 4th century, army commanders received the title duke (*dux*), while that of count (*comes*) was conferred on a whole range of officials. The Latin language would transmit and perpetuate these titles into times which would endow them with quite different significance. The word 'aristocracy', meanwhile, disappeared from regular usage for around a thousand years. When it resurfaced, in the 15th century, it still meant a form of government, but it was largely employed to describe states ruled by noblemen.

The term 'noble' had never fallen out of usage, at least among the Latinate clerics who composed the records of medieval times. They used it to describe the secular elites of post-classical Europe, families who revered good birth as much as the ancients. But there was no sense among medieval nobles of the civic-minded virtue that Aristotle or his Roman disciples thought marked out the best people. Certainly they had wealth to sustain their pretensions, but what they respected above all was fighting. Nobility now meant prowess on the battlefield. The conventional medieval description of society divided it into three groups. Written down by clerics, it naturally assigned the prime function to the clergy: those who prayed. But a close second came those who fought: the nobility. The rest simply worked. As a description of reality, this was never watertight. By the time it crystallized, there were already nobles who did not fight, and their numbers would swell steadily over subsequent centuries. But in several kingdoms, the tripartite division of social functions provided justification for a formal organization into legally constituted orders, often with their own forms of institutional representation. And the warrior vocation remained a crucial element in the definition and identity of nobilities from barbarian times right down to the 20th century.

Just like the ancient elites to whom educated nobles instinctively compared themselves, they naturally assumed they were the best people. But few of them lived in aristocratic states as originally defined. Apart from a handful of mostly Italian city-states collectively governed, like the republics of antiquity, by hereditary elites, most governments were now monarchies. And although monarchs generally held and transmitted their thrones by the same hereditary principles as nobles, it took time to establish the idea that even under a single ruler power was effectively shared. The final breakthrough occurred only in 1748, when Montesquieu formally abandoned the Aristotelian taxonomy of states. For him, in *The Spirit of the Laws*, the three basic types were republics, monarchies, and despotisms. An aristocracy was merely one type of republic, where the few governed rather than the many. He identified these ruling minorities as nobles, but the true destiny of nobles for Montesquieu lay in monarchies. There they played an essential role as an intermediary power between monarch and subjects, upholding the laws and preventing the state's degeneration into despotism. His fundamental maxim was 'no monarch, no nobility; no nobility, no monarch'.

But once kings and nobles were convincingly shown to stand together, it became possible to think of them falling together, too. When, only three decades after Montesquieu wrote, the American revolutionaries successfully renounced allegiance to George III and established a republic, they declared that any form of nobility was incompatible with their new state. They also began to talk about the dangers of 'an aristocracy' of the rich usurping power – thus eliding Aristotle's careful distinction between aristocracy and oligarchy. And around 1780, while the issue in America was still unresolved, reformers in the Dutch Republic began to denounce their own oligarchs as *aristocrats*– a word previously unknown. Within a few years, it was taken up by the French revolutionaries to describe their own opponents. This usage derived from the fact that the Revolution had begun as a struggle to destroy the privileges and power of the French nobility. Aristocracy now clearly meant more than just a form of government. It meant the power of a particular social group and its supporters. It also meant that group itself in a more general way. Aristocracy and nobility had at last become completely interchangeable as descriptive terms.

This has been the common usage ever since. Some analysts or commentators employ the word 'aristocracy' to make distinctions within the wider ranks of nobles, confining the term to the rich minority of influential magnates or peers. This can be useful for certain sorts of analysis, but in more general terms the description 'aristocratic', or the nouns 'aristocrat' or 'aristocracy', are widely (if imprecisely) understood to mean much the same thing as noble or nobility.

Both are terms for European elites. But Europeans in their encounters with other cultures have instinctively reached for their own categories to understand what they found there. Accordingly, 'aristocracy' or 'nobility' have been employed to describe oligarchic governments and social elites far beyond the confines of Europe. But while all aristocracies are elites, not all elites are aristocracies, and non-European versions need to be defined and described on their own terms, which would demand a different sort of book. This one, accordingly, confines itself to European experience. Even then, almost anything we can say by way of definition will prove subject to exceptions. Nevertheless, certain broad principles seem to cover most cases.

Nobility

Nobility has always meant public distinction, from the 'known' families of ancient Rome to those who figured until 1944 in the revered German *Almanach de Gotha*, or still today in the French *Bottin mondain*, or *Burke's Peerage* or *Landed Gentry*. People invested with nobility enjoy an acknowledged superiority – whether acknowledgement comes from the rest of society, from others like themselves, from public authorities, or most often from all three at once. There is no objective or scientific basis for it. 'Blue blood', a quality first claimed by Christian warriors in medieval Castile and often invoked subsequently as shorthand for nobility, was never more than a colourful metaphor. Candid observers, even in times when noble authority was unchallenged, admitted that in the end nobility was nothing more than a figment of opinion or belief. It was no less persuasive for that, bolstered as it usually has been by a whole range of more tangible claims to superiority.

How is this elusive and exclusive distinction acquired? Historically, there have been three ways.

For much of the Middle Ages, nobles were recruited by osmosis and absorption. Families acquired recognition as noble by building up a range of attributes and activities recognized as appropriate – amassing land and dependants, demonstrating martial skills and achievements, and generally 'living nobly' (see Chapter 3). This way of asserting claims to nobility has never entirely died out, and few families have ever become noble without first establishing the elements of a noble lifestyle. But from the late 15th to the 19th centuries (and sometimes beyond), to claim nobility entirely on this basis was regarded as usurpation. It continued to occur, but became much harder to carry off. This was because, during those centuries, rulers established an effective monopoly of ennoblement. In implicit return for the recognition or grant of privileges, nobles allowed kings (or sovereign assemblies in the few remaining republics, like Venice or Genoa) to take control of entry to their ranks.

Secondly, therefore, nobility has been conferred by grant of the sovereign. The most incontrovertible entitlement or 'proof' is a patent or letters of nobility issued in due form by the competent authority. Nearly all noble lineages are traceable back to such a document, and even those claiming to be older are based on authenticated recognition by such an authority of pre-existing nobility. The ways and grounds for official ennoblement are very diverse. Monarchs have never been answerable for their motivations in conferring the status, although they might incur bitter criticism if they raised up favourites, as it was invariably put, 'from the dust'. Most often, ennoblement was granted in recognition of service, whether on the battlefield or, increasingly, in politics or administration. Ennoblement of administrators was mostly automatic: upon reaching a certain level, the distinction came *ex officio*. But letters of appointment still confirmed the new status.

Thirdly, nobility could be bought. It was seldom openly sold, except in times of financial emergency, but in practice few families ever achieved ennoblement without paying out substantial sums. Rulers recognized from an early stage that distinctions had a lucrative market value, and that the monopoly of issuing them could be an important source of revenue. Thus patents were never issued unaccompanied by a range of fees. And in France, where between the late 15th century and the Revolution of 1789 most crown offices were for sale, several thousand of the highest and most expensive ones conferred ennoblement.

Yet few nobilities saw themselves as creations of the state. Another term often used interchangeably with nobility is 'gentility'. Nobles were gentlemen, and only in the course of the 18th century did that word come to lose in English the meaning which it retained in Latin languages as exclusively someone of 'gentle' birth. Birth was the best entitlement of all: true gentlemen were begotten, not made. As Francis I of France (1515–47) is reputed to have declared, the king could create as many noblemen as he liked, but never a gentleman.

Heredity

Aristocracies are hereditary elites. They pass on their distinction down the generations, and inherit the noble blood of their forefathers. Bloodline, breeding, even race, are terms regularly found in theoretical discussions of what nobility is or was. Personal nobility is not unknown: it was found in the Table of Ranks for state servants established in Russia by Peter the Great in 1722, or the somewhat similar titular hierarchy created by Napoleon for his empire in 1808. But both creations were pervaded by the assumption that hereditary distinction was still a more desirable ideal, and that personal ennoblement was simply a way-station on the road to full heredity – as it had been in pre-revolutionary France, where most ennobling offices required three successive generations of occupancy to confer full transmissible nobility. Only the life peerages created in Great Britain from 1958, in the twilight of the old House of Lords, carried no presumption whatsoever of inheritance. An Act of 1963 introduced another novel principle: hereditary peers might now renounce their peerages. Normally, as

2. A great nobleman and his family: Philip Herbert, fourth Earl of Pembroke, by Van Dyck, Wilton House, Wiltshire

a genetically transmitted quality, nobility has been inalienable. Noble children have a right to their father's status, provided that they are born in wedlock. Kings almost always ennobled their illegitimate children, but noble bastards usually enjoyed no more patrimonial rights than illegitimate commoners, although nobles were often in a position to solicit special exemptions.

Yet in certain circumstances nobility might be lost. A nobleman convicted of treason might be stripped of his rank or at least the property that sustained it. More usually, the status might be lost if its holder engaged in activities deemed incompatible with nobility. In France, this was called derogation (*dérogeance*) and was incurred if a nobleman undertook manual labour or retail trade. The hand that held the sword, the maxim ran, could not also hold a purse; or, as an early 17th-century treatise put it, 'It is base and sordid gain that derogates from nobility. The proper course for nobility is to live on one's rents, or at least not to sell one's efforts or one's labour.' Laws enshrining this principle were rarely flouted. They were underpinned by powerful prejudices against demeaning occupations which long outlasted the lapse of formal prohibitions in the later 18th century.

If heredity is central to the aristocratic ideal, there has been enormous variety in the way it has been practised. Mostly, it has been patrilinear: nobility passed on through the male rather than the female line. Influential families again might win special dispensations; but whereas the children of a noble father and a non-noble woman would be born noble, those of a noblewoman marrying a commoner would inherit the paternal status. In most cases, all legitimate children of a noble father are born equally noble. The most celebrated exceptions are in the three kingdoms of Great Britain, where peers alone count as noblemen and only the eldest son, or a younger brother if he dies childless, inherits the status ('the heir and the spare'). All other children are legally commoners, inheriting nothing but the right to display the family coat of arms. Yet in real terms, the British aristocracies have always been wider than the peerage. The baronetage, whose titles are transmissible on the same terms as peerages, and the far more numerous gentry – the gentle-born, after all – have always been the obvious equivalent of Continental lesser nobles. On his Grand Tour in 1764, James Boswell, later famous as the biographer of Samuel Johnson but then merely the son of a Scottish judge and landowner, decided that 'I think proper to take the title of Baron in Germany, as I have just the same right to it as the good gentry I see around me'. Nevertheless, British primogeniture inexorably thrust younger siblings out of the aristocratic elites at every level, forcing them to compete, as Continental noble offspring need not, to keep bright the reflected glory of distinguished ancestors. But only by starting a new line could they hope to recover the status of their forefathers. The most vivid example is perhaps the Duke of Wellington, younger son of an earl, who achieved a peerage himself only through his exploits on the battlefield.

A single male ancestor is enough to establish a noble line. Only the death of all direct male descendants can extinguish it. But not all

3. Decaying squire courts young bride with his family tree: detail from William Hogarth's *Marriage à la mode*

bloodlines are equally pure. The oldest nobility, lost in the mists of time, is enjoyed by families whose first known ancestor was already recognized as noble. All other lines begin, however remotely, with someone who was not born noble, but achieved the status in his lifetime. Accordingly, the prestige of a line reflects the length of ancestry and the number of noble generations. A further criterion, essential in Germany though simply desirable elsewhere, is the number of noble ancestors on the maternal as much as the paternal side. From outside, aristocracies can appear uniform and monolithic in their exclusivity. There is nothing equal about their internal arrangements.

Hierarchy

The essence of aristocracy is inequality. It rests on the presumption that some people are naturally better than most others. But if nobles are better than commoners, nobles are profoundly differentiated among themselves. Nor is the disdain of any noble for ancestry more recent than his or her own simply a matter of family pride, without material consequences. Many prestigious institutions, such as courts, chapters, monasteries, orders of chivalry, regiments, or schools, have limited their recruitment to nobles enjoying a specified minimum length of proven pedigree. Length of lineage might also dictate public precedence, especially among nobles with no titles to distinguish them. An extreme case was Russia, where in the 16th and 17th centuries titles were almost unknown, but the tenure of any office was dependent on *mestnichestvo*, a system whereby nobody could be outranked by anybody with an ancestor who had served at a lower level. It was a formula for paralysis, and was abolished in 1682. Yet only 40 years later, a new scale of ranks and titles was instituted.

Contrary to a widespread belief, in the history of aristocracy titles are a relative rarity, and a relatively late arrival. The titles bestowed by the later Roman emperors were not resurrected in the West for many centuries after the empire's collapse, although they lingered on in the shrunken empire ruled from Constantinople. In the early medieval West, dukes and counts were almost always magnates of royal blood. Only in the 12th and 13th centuries did a hierarchy of titles begin to establish itself, with the creation of the first non-royal dukes. They were held to outrank holders of existing established titles like count or (English equivalent) earl, a superiority generally underpinned by greater wealth. By the 15th century, hierarchies of hereditary titles were emerging all over Western Europe, as kings rewarded the loyalty of influential subjects by carefully calibrating the scale of their importance. There were now marquesses between dukes and counts, while viscounts came between the latter and relatively lowly barons. Matters were particularly complex in Germany, where for a thousand years before its dissolution in 1806 the highest level of authority was the Holy Roman Empire. It was the legitimating source of a high imperial nobility, some of whom were effectively sovereign princes enjoying a vote in the election of the emperor, ruling extensive territories themselves; and so-called free imperial knights without territorial attributions, though seldom without extensive private estates. At the same time, German sovereign princes like the electors of Brandenburg (later kings of Prussia) stood at the head of nobilities of their own, lower in prestige than imperial nobles but sometimes far richer. In most nobilities, titles were passed on in the male line, and were tied to particular landed endowments or lordships, which if alienated took the title with them. Only in the British monarchies did title become divorced from territory and jurisdiction. In the later Middle Ages, too, peerages began to be established, exclusive groups of magnates with special privileges not shared (except in Great Britain) by other title-holders: the 'dukes and peers' of France, the grandees of Spain, the barons of Naples and Sicily.

But simply because titles initially derived from substantial accumulations of wealth, the vast majority of nobles could never aspire to them; and a prestigious title bore no necessary correlation to length of lineage. Many an impoverished squire took solace in sneering at the flawed and recent ancestry of titled neighbours. Meanwhile, they sought to advertise their own status with lesser embellishments. There were simple knighthoods, titles granted strictly for life, but generally accorded only to gentlemen. 'Esquire' (literally 'shield-bearer') was widely used to make claims to gentility and to say 'this man has a coat of arms'. On the Continent (and to some extent in Scotland), the most recognizable sign was the use of the particle, the telltale *de*, *von*, or *of* in front of the last name, implying lordship of a noble estate. Many polite forms of address (Sir, *Monsieur*, *Herr*, *Signor*, *Señor*) began as terms of deference to such social superiors.

Within the ranks of most aristocracies, therefore, hierarchical differences between their members were almost as important as what distinguished them from the rest of society. But not all embraced formal hierarchies (as opposed to differences in wealth) without resistance. In the Italian city republics, and among the most numerous nobility in Europe, that of Poland, the equality of all nobles was fiercely defended. What titles existed in the Polish commonwealth were of foreign origin, acknowledged out of courtesy rather than enshrined in law. And it took determined action by resolute rulers to impose titular hierarchies in Hungary, Russia, and Prussia over the early modern centuries. But kings knew that hierarchy was a system of control, just like the wider web of privilege in which nobles jostled to participate.

Privilege

Privilege means 'private law'. Those who have it enjoy the right to be treated differently from others. The idea of aristocracy or nobility without privilege is inconceivable. It is often said that what distinguishes the nobility of the British kingdoms from their Continental counterparts is that they have had no privileges. They have certainly always had fewer. But if we accept the peculiar

British definition of nobility as the peerage, then membership of the House of Lords, to which all peers were entitled until 1999, has certainly been a privilege of the first importance. Even if we prefer a wider definition of the British aristocracy, the hereditary title of baronet, knighthoods, and the coats of arms which gentlemen are entitled to display, not to mention the public precedence which the gentry traditionally took immediately behind peers, are aristocratic privileges too. Between 1711 and 1858, men without substantial landed estates were formally excluded from the House of Commons; and from 1671 to 1832, the game laws effectively banned all but the gentry from hunting and shooting.

Hunting privileges were a lordly monopoly throughout Europe. So was the right to certain sorts of coats of arms – although non-nobles were often entitled to display less distinctive armorial bearings. Much more important, many Continental nobilities had been constituted by the later Middle Ages into separate legal orders enjoying collective rights and privileges, often including their own chambers in representative institutions. The rationale for this was their separate function as the warriors who notionally offered protection to the community. In Poland and Hungary, only nobles enjoyed representation of any sort. Even more significant, the presumed warrior vocation of nobles served as justification for exemption from direct taxation. Nobles paid the 'blood tax' and therefore felt entitled to pay no other. One of the long-running themes of early modern history is the constant effort of kings to subject nobles, generally the richest category of their subjects, to taxation. Sooner or later, ways were usually found to tap their wealth indirectly. Direct taxation, however, was fiercely resisted, not only because of the claims it made on noble wealth, but because tax-exemption was the acid test of nobility itself. 'No noble is taxable' (*taillable*) ran the French maxim, and it took the greatest revolution in history to destroy this principle.

And yet, by 1789, the king's struggle to tap noble wealth was half won. French nobles already paid a range of indirect taxes, and in parts of the kingdom the touchstone tax, the *taille*, was in any case levied on land rather than persons. Classification of land into noble and non-noble was widespread across the Continent, and in some countries only nobles were allowed to acquire noble lands. Even where commoners were not debarred, a special tax (*franc-fief*) was payable on their acquisitions. Meanwhile, nobles enjoyed all sorts of other exemptions, although these varied widely from one kingdom to another. They included exemptions from billeting, from militia service, and from corporal punishment. Capital punishment was by decapitation rather than by hanging. Cases involving nobles were often tried in special courts, and a wide range of institutions and corporate bodies were closed to anybody but the nobility. Noblemen, finally, were entitled to look different. If sumptuary laws enacted between the 14th and 17th centuries largely failed to prevent rich commoners from dressing like their betters, only the most presumptuous dared to flout laws which confined sword-bearing to nobles. This was another way of flaunting the warrior vocation, and it presupposed some training in swordplay which commoners might be unable to match if weapons were drawn.

Privileges originated in many different ways. Some, like political representation or tax-exemption, were integral to the concept of nobility. Others were granted by kings to gain support or in capitulation to concerted opposition. Still others were simply sold – a less painful way for rulers to tap wealth than trying to enforce taxes when their coercive power was limited. The British rank of baronet, allowing hereditary transmission of the title 'Sir', was created in 1611 explicitly for sale, although subsequently it was granted in return for political services. The French crown, meanwhile, sold public offices with privileges attached, including ennoblement on a scale which transformed the whole character of the French nobility over three centuries before the Revolution from a warrior elite into an open plutocracy. But privileges conceded or sold were seldom acquired by whole orders of nobility. They were granted piecemeal, to subgroups or successions of individuals, reinforcing or modifying existing hierarchies to the ultimate advantage of royal power. The result was that a minority of aristocrats always found themselves with far more privileges than the rest; and this uneven distribution of advantages only compounded snobberies and antagonisms between nobles which made the external appearance of aristocratic solidarity a fragile illusion.

Duties

Privileges were rights. They were enshrined in law and protected by the courts. Nobles never hesitated to undertake litigation to uphold them, for they were essential appurtenances of aristocratic claims to social superiority. By contrast, the prescribed duties of nobles were minimal and altogether vaguer. In the West, they mostly derived from the heyday of feudalism, between the 10th and the 13th centuries. The word 'feudalism' was scarcely used before the 17th century, and modern scholars prefer to avoid it. Yet the fief (*feudum*) so characteristic of that period, and the laws and customs deriving from it, were to mark almost every aspect of aristocratic history down to the end of the 18th century and sometimes beyond. Fiefs were conditional grants of lands and jurisdiction from a lord to a contracting subordinate or vassal. They often included a central strong-point where a castle could be constructed. But the essence of the feudal contract was that a vassal would provide the lord on demand with an agreed number of mounted warriors, called on the Continent 'horsemen' (*caballarius, caballero, chevalier, Ritter*) and in England, 'knights'. Fiefs varied in size according to the number of knights they were expected to provide, but feudatories (fief-holders) who failed to meet their engagements might legitimately be dispossessed. Castles and knights dominated warfare from the 10th to the 14th centuries, but with the arrival of new battlefield tactics and (a century later) gunpowder, feudal arrangements began to fade. The lethal knightly pastime of jousting continued well into the 16th century, but when occasionally in the 17th a feudal host was still called up, the results

4. Jousting knights, 15th century

were seen as little more than an amateur embarrassment. But by then, titles derived from castles, knighthood as an honoured vocation, armorial bearings (originally for recognition in battle), a complex jurisprudence of fiefs and the jurisdiction that went with them, and the code of proper knightly behaviour known as chivalry, were all part of the very fabric of noble identity. From it derived the notion that a nobleman owed service to his supreme lord, the king – a sense of obligation that survived in a widespread commitment to military careers far into the 19th century and beyond.

Not all nobles shared this sense. The teeming nobility of early modern Poland, the famous *Szlachta*, counted exemption from military service as one of their privileges. They gloried in having no obligations to anybody but themselves and called it 'golden freedom'. Further east, on the anarchic steppe frontier, this was a luxury that nobody could afford. Russian nobles were always known as slaves or servitors of the Czar. Like earlier feudal vassals in the West, they enjoyed the grant of land and serfs to work it for their maintenance, but their obligation to serve was much more open-ended. Certainly most of their service was military, but they were completely at the disposal of the ruler for whatever purpose and for entirely as long as he liked. Peter the Great (1682–1725) extended and systematized this principle, requiring all nobles to serve for life either in the army or as 'civil servants' (the first use of this term). This regime proved transient. The state could not use all the lifetime servitors which it provided, and in 1762 nobles acquired the right to leave service. But by then, most did not know what else to do, and the return of many of them to their estates and a closer exploitation of their serfs exacerbated social tensions in the countryside. There followed massive popular uprisings in the 1770s, and a shaken Catherine the Great (1762–96) sought to woo the loyalty of the nobility by a comprehensive grant of privileges. The Charter of the Nobility in 1785 gave Russian nobles advantages and exemptions on a scale that was by then beginning to be eroded in Western Europe. It was designed to make them eager to serve the government at every level, but without any of the old compulsion. And since it guaranteed their properties and their holdings of serfs, and gave them an institutional say in local government, Russian nobles took very little persuading to offer their services voluntarily.

Aristocrats have never taken kindly to compulsion. They have seen themselves as born to command others rather than accept the dictates of superiors. The duty of higher authority in their eyes has been to confirm and uphold their pretensions. Even acceptance of royal supremacy has seldom been more than conditional. Few put it as vividly or explicitly as the medieval notables of Barcelona, who swore to their Aragonese monarch that:

> We, who are as good as you, swear to you, who are no better than
> us, to accept you as our king and sovereign, provided that you
> observe all our liberties and laws, but if not, not.

Nevertheless, this has never been far from the aristocratic attitude. History is littered with noble or baronial revolts against authority, not to mention the overthrow and murder of rulers by discontented noblemen. For the conduct, rights, and duties of aristocracies have been laid down far less in formal rules and definitions than in what their members have chosen to believe about themselves.

Chapter 2
Myths and beliefs

If aristocracies can be objectively defined as hierarchical elites legally enjoying hereditary nobility and a variable range of privileges and public obligations, they have always sought to define themselves further in terms of beliefs and behaviour. To an astonishing degree, outsiders, whether contemporaries or historians, have been prepared to accept and perpetuate nobles' own versions of who they are, where they came from, what they do, and what they deserve. Even critics of aristocracy have tended to frame their opposition in terms of its failure to live up to its own idealized identity.

Origins

Aristocracies believe they have existed since time immemorial. They see themselves as manifestations and beneficiaries of a natural human tendency to accept the leadership of elites of proven superiority. When noblemen spoke of themselves, as they so often did, as patricians or senators, they were implying that they were the same sort of people as the rulers of ancient Rome. A few even claimed direct descent from at least the senatorial order of late antiquity. Most modern aristocracies, however, have traced their collective identity no further back than the upheavals of the barbarian invasions in the early Middle Ages. Some saw themselves as descendants of conquerors, with conquest as the ultimate proof and justification of their superiority. The nobles of the Polish Commonwealth (before it disappeared in 1795) monopolized power more completely than any of their counterparts across Europe. They did so as self-proclaimed descendants of 'Sarmatians' who were supposed to have conquered and enserfed the previous inhabitants around the end of the first millennium. The Hungarian nobility to the south made somewhat more credible claims of descent from the Magyars who had terrorized Eastern Europe around the same time. At the other end of the Continent, all legitimate authority and property in England could be traced back to the Norman Conquest of 1066, following which William I redistributed the lands of the former English elites to his leading collaborators. Some early modern French writers argued that the origins of their own nobility lay in the twilight of the Roman Empire centuries earlier, depicting them as descendants of the Franks who, under Clovis (c. 466–511), supplanted the Romans as lords of the indigenous Gauls.

Few of these claims can withstand scholarly scrutiny. Some, like the idea of Frankish conquest, were contentious almost from the moment they were first propounded. Much about the origins of modern European nobilities still is. But even if the idea of tribal conquest is simplistic, at least it seems clear that nobilities emerged and evolved in the crucible of medieval warfare and the need to provide material support for mounted warriors. In the West, the trappings and terminology of feudalism, whose relics mark so much of the aristocratic ethos, came together at much the same time as triumphant Sarmatians and Magyars were supposedly settling further east. The scanty and often ambiguous chronicles of these times gave plenty of scope for the invention or embroidery of heroic ancestors. So did the Crusades of the 11th and 12th centuries, when knights could make fabulous reputations in the highest of all Christian quests – the capture, defence, and then attempted recapture of the Holy Land. One of the most exclusive orders of chivalry, the Knights of St John of Jerusalem, who retained an independent headquarters on the island of Malta until

1798, traced its origin back to that time. Glorious forebears could also be found among the Teutonic Knights who sought to Christianize the east Baltic shore by the sword in the 13th century, or the heroes of the centuries-long reconquest of the Iberian peninsula from the Muslims. Exclusive and self-recruiting orders of chivalry perpetuated the memory of these campaigns far into religiously less militant centuries. But when, at the end of the 18th, aristocracy came under open attack, gleeful opponents found the idea of nobility deriving from conquest irresistible for turning the tables on nobles. The supposed triumph of the Franks, or in England the 'Norman Yoke', could then be depicted as alien assaults on older native freedoms.

Not many noble families could credibly trace a continuous line of ancestry to really remote times, but the dream of long generations of glorious or heroic forebears was pervasive. Nobles treasure their family trees, and genealogists have always made a good living producing them to order. They are not in business to disprove the claims of those who hire them, and false or fabricated lineages litter the annals of aristocratic pride. Nor is private gratification the only point. Almost as important as age in family trees is alliances: inter-marriage with families of similar if not greater distinction. The aristocratic marriage market depends on the 'extraction' of potential spouses being known, and the more exclusive nobilities, like those of Germany, set less store by generations of male ancestors than by 'quarterings' – unsullied nobility in ancestors of both sexes, symbolized by subdivisions in coats of arms. Enjoyment of certain privileges has also often depended on an acceptable genealogy. By the 16th century, rulers were increasingly keeping their own records of noble credentials, entrusted to the care of heralds, judges of arms, or court genealogists. The job of such officials was as much to challenge as to confirm lineages, since states and institutions of exclusive recruitment had no interest in the over-proliferation of privilege. When, with the shrinkage of aristocratic privileges over the 19th century, states lost interest in tracking those entitled to them, the

5. Armorial bearings with 16 quarterings: a heraldic banner, Trerice, Cornwall

task was taken up by the publishers of 'nobiliaries', almanacs and reference books, not all of whom have been equally scrupulous in recording or admitting ancestral claims. But even the most rigorous, such as the German *Almanach de Gotha* published annually between 1763 and 1944, have been subject to constant complaints and criticism over omissions or contested entries. Nobles are notoriously more interested in what flatters their vanity than in documentary truth or accuracy.

Nothing compares in noble ideas of distinction to an unbroken line of male descent. But nothing is rarer. In demographic terms, the likelihood that any family will produce surviving male heirs much beyond three successive generations is extremely small. Aristocratic priorities have a tendency to diminish it yet further: family sizes have often been deliberately limited in order to protect property from the claims of too many heirs, and the warrior vocation of noblemen exposes them to increased risks. Sooner or later, even fertile marriages produce only daughters; and the line disappears, unless an heiress marries a cousin with the same name, or her husband changes his own name to hers. Many of the proudest lineages owe their survival to such strategies, but the majority of noble families have always been doomed to extinction after only a few generations. Certainly this can only enhance the prestige of the ever-dwindling handful of families whose lineage is ancient and unbroken; but for most, at any given moment a long pedigree can be no more than myth or wishful thinking. Equally mythical therefore is the social exclusivity of aristocracies. Any group so demographically fragile can only survive by full and regular transfusions of new blood. Even where their ranks were officially closed, as in the hallowed republic of Venice, the 'Golden Book' in which all noble families were officially recorded was periodically, if briefly, opened to allow the shrinking ranks of the elite to be replenished. Aristocratic castes without machinery for legitimate admission of newcomers can only wither away. That is what is happening today, when authentic ennoblement no longer occurs anywhere, not even in Great Britain. The effect, of course, is to make the ranks of recognized nobles ever more exclusive – so long as they last.

Recruitment

Although birth is enough to confer nobility, aristocrats have normally been reluctant to admit that nobility signifies no other qualities. They like to think that their ancestors earned their distinction by deeds of valour, virtue, and outstanding service to king and/or community. They like to think that these propensities are to some extent hereditary, or at least reflect well on descendants. They generally admit that they have no monopoly on such qualities, although they tend to believe that they are more likely to be found among people of their own sort, that 'social advantages were rightfully imparted by inheritance rather than performance'. Some have even been prepared to accept that commoners who demonstrate the right qualities might deserve ennoblement in recognition. But few aristocrats have cared to concede that wealth is any sort of qualification for joining their ranks.

In practice, nothing has been more important. If the origins of nobility were in one way or another military, they reflected the growing expense of being battle-ready. And if since medieval times successful soldiers and sailors from lowly backgrounds have sometimes fought their way to nobility, they have seldom done so without amassing fortunes in booty or prizes on the way. For most of its history, directly or indirectly, entry to nobility has been bought, and in social terms, one of aristocracy's main historic functions has been to make new money respectable. It is true that open and outright purchase has been the exception. 'Cash for honours' has never been thought legitimate, and there was widespread shock when Louis XIV sold titles and patents of nobility in the 1690s, or that nemesis of the House of Lords, David Lloyd George, sold peerages to bolster his party's funds in the 1920s. On the eve of the Revolution, a good two-thirds of the French nobility was descended from office-holders ennobled by a purchase over the preceding two centuries. But there are more ways of buying nobility than direct purchase. Noblemen anxious to refurbish their fortunes have seldom hesitated to seek out and marry the daughters of moneyed commoners offering substantial dowries. It was called 'regilding the arms' or, less politely, 'restoring the fields with muck', but it kept replenished not only noble wealth but also the aristocratic gene pool. In any case, being noble is expensive. Nobody without substantial wealth could dream of sustaining the status, and rulers were normally careful to ennoble nobody too poor to keep it up. When in 1808 Napoleon decided to create a titled aristocracy to decorate his upstart imperial pretensions, he specified a minimum level of opulence for each gradation on his scale of dignities. In previous centuries, more legitimate monarchs in both England and France had periodically tried to force non-noble subjects of substantial fortune to upgrade themselves into knighthood or nobility – although this was also a way of tapping their wealth by charging them for the elevation. But few men of the requisite level of fortune needed to be given such incentives. They would already have drawn attention to themselves by investing their resources in land rather than leaving them liquid and hidden; and this alone would suggest that they harboured social ambitions.

Joining an aristocracy is never accomplished quickly. However acquired, a formal grant of nobility is only one step along the way, though doubtless the most important. Investing in land, that quintessential noble asset, is another. But only acceptance by other members of the elite signals a process of absorption successfully completed. A common adage was that it took three generations to make a gentleman; and even then there was no way of measuring it objectively. Eventually, however, time would do its work. A moneyed newcomer would find noble suitors for his daughters, and marriage would bring ties of kinship. The elements of the aristocratic lifestyle would be observantly aped, sons would be placed in noble employments, and over time humble origins could be blurred and hopefully forgotten. Qualities painstakingly learned could now be taken as innate.

Survival

Nobility is for ever. Individuals may forfeit it in certain clearly defined circumstances, but a quality passed on in the blood cannot be expunged – as the French revolutionaries found when they tried in 1790 to abolish it. As one outraged victim then put it, nobles 'would not believe that any human power could prevent them from passing on to their descendants the quality of *gentleman*, which they had received *only from God*'. The supreme private duty of a firstborn nobleman is to perpetuate the line, and thereby enhance in the future a family lustre inherited from the past. But maintaining the glory of a family credibly depends on conserving adequate material resources, and much in aristocratic circumstances made this difficult.

In most countries, all children inherited the paternal status. Even in England, where titles were passed on by strict male primogeniture, younger children of a titled father retained the family coat of arms and sometimes, for one generation, a courtesy title. But whereas in England property, too, was inherited by primogeniture until 1925, and younger children had no legal claim upon it, in most Continental countries the basic laws guaranteed every child a portion of parental goods. The precise portion might vary widely, from full equality (widespread in Eastern Europe), to a share dwarfed by that of the eldest son or preferred testamentary heir. The inevitable effect, however, was to split up family properties every generation, and to leave many heirs with patrimony that was scarcely viable. English cadets did not even have that, and without guaranteed resources, were thrust down into the ranks of commoners. Meanwhile, their Continental counterparts and their descendants, prohibited by law, prejudice, or both from turning to trade to maintain their fortunes, could find themselves marooned in modest or downright straitened circumstances constantly felt to be unworthy of their status. In the British Isles, really poor nobles scarcely existed: they sank into the commonalty. On the Continent, they posed a social problem that came to preoccupy governments more and more between the 16th and the 19th centuries.

None of this invalidates the conventional picture of vast and far-flung noble estates governed from great houses. These could be found in most countries before the 20th century. But, eye-catching though they were, and the mansions and castles which they once sustained still are, they were only enjoyed by a minority, and even here the prestige of the head of the family was only maintained at the expense of younger siblings. An extreme case was the British Isles, where estate concentration was favoured by primogeniture, and was reinforced in the 17th and 18th centuries by widespread use of the 'strict settlement', a form of entail which restricted the free disposal of a family patrimony by any heir over three generations. But even in lands without primogeniture, or where it was confined (as in France) to the transmission of fiefs and associated titles, it was sometimes possible at great expense to set up entails. In Spain, the *mayorazgo*, in southern Italy and the Habsburg lands, the *fideicommissum*, held vast family estates together down the generations, however badly any head of the family managed them. After the French Revolution had demonstrated the vulnerability of nobilities, there were moves to help them resist the break-up of estates. Prussian nobles abandoned their long-standing commitment to partible inheritance, and took out increasing numbers of entails right down to 1914. Napoleon encouraged his new titled hierarchy to protect their landed wealth through *majorats*. The restored Bourbons maintained the practice, and even tried in 1826 to generalize primogeniture for the richest families – although this proved a step too far for that majority who still lived in modest circumstances.

They still preferred more traditional strategies for staving off impoverishment. Family size could be artificially limited, thus reducing the number of possible claims on parental estates. There is some evidence from the 17th century onwards that this was beginning to happen. The larger portions which surviving children then inherited would give them better hopes of increasing them further by advantageous marriages with counterparts similarly placed. In Catholic countries before the French Revolution, the richer benefices, chapters, and monasteries of the Church were extensively colonized by aristocratic scions making no further claims on their families; and even in post-Reformation England by the 18th century many a rural parson was a younger brother of the squire. Younger sons might also dream of living up to their ancestors through that quintessentially aristocratic vocation, a military career. The legendary army of Frederick the Great was officered by noblemen reared on the poor and constantly subdivided soil of Brandenburg and Prussia. Further west, however, army officers were recruited by purchase – in France until the eve of the Revolution, in Great Britain until 1871 – and this effectively excluded many who believed that background and family traditions made them obvious candidates for leading men into battle. Worst placed of all in families of modest means were sisters. Without adequate dowries, they were unmarriageable. Even nunneries often demanded dowries for entry. Accordingly, daughters were commonly regarded in aristocratic families at any level of wealth as a misfortune – a drain on family finances whether they married or not, and either way doing nothing to perpetuate the family name.

Yet the most obvious ways to avoid impoverishment were the ones nobles shunned. As landowners, they might have taken to exploiting their most substantial assets directly, and in innovative ways; and where agricultural innovations did occur, noblemen were more often than not responsible. Everybody has heard of the 18th-century innovations in England of Viscount 'Turnip' Townshend. Nevertheless, these were exceptions. The vast majority of nobles preferred to live off agriculture indirectly through rents or the dues and services of serfs. And even where they were not formally prohibited from trading by laws of derogation, nobles were reluctant to soil their hands with commerce. Eighteenth-century governments were keen to dispel this prejudice. The king of France repeatedly urged his nobles into wholesale trade, at least by making it non-derogatory. The Russian charter of nobility of 1785 explicitly authorized nobles to enter commerce. And in all sorts of roundabout ways, often deliberately disguised, nobles with capital to invest were happy enough to reap the rewards of placing it commercially, in trade or in finance. Modern research is increasingly revealing the economic reach of 'gentlemanly capitalism'. The problem for poor nobles, however, was precisely the lack of any sort of capital. Too many noble families had initially achieved their status by abandoning the 'counting house', and to go back to it was an admission of social failure. In pre-revolutionary Brittany, impoverished nobles could 'put their nobility to sleep' while they refurbished their family fortunes in trade, resuming it when the damage was repaired. But this was quite exceptional. The poorer the noble, in fact, the more likely he was to despise and avoid the commercial stigma, disdaining the only avenue leading out of genteel penury. A long literary tradition mocked this behaviour. The antics of *Don Quixote* (1605–15), threadbare but obsessed with knightly conduct, were translated into every major European language. Yet as a French legal commentator observed around the time this great satire was written, 'Poverty is no vice, and does not denoble.' It simply set up tensions between means and expectations which nothing could resolve. A century and a half later, the problem was no nearer solution. As the Marquis de Mirabeau, father of the notorious renegade orator of the French Revolution, wrote in 1756, 'Without money, honour is nothing but a sickness.'

Honour

Nobles have always thought of themselves above all as honourable. This means entitled to public recognition, but also obliged to act in such a way as to deserve it. But honour was one of those qualities which everybody could recognize but few found easy to define. Much of the notion is traceable back to the ideals of chivalry which emerged in the high Middle Ages to guide the conduct of knights. Knighthood originated as a formal military vocation. Accordingly its most prized quality was courage, and boldness in combat. The most vaunted exploits of noble ancestors were achieved on the battlefield, and the ultimate dishonour was cowardice. Long after mounted knights had ceased to dominate warfare, exclusive orders of knighthood or chivalry, with special costumes, ribbons, and insignia, were among the most coveted distinctions. New ones continued to be established for centuries. Even the knightly pastime of jousting, supremely violent and dangerous, only died out long after it had lost all military value. And not until the early 19th century did noblemen cease to carry swords in everyday life as a mark of their willingness to fight to defend their honour. Duelling, which pitted like against like in single combat, originated as a judicial way of settling disputes between knights. When lawyers abandoned it for the more prosaic processes of litigation, noblemen continued to favour duels in matters of honour down to the early 20th century. Nobles attracted no shame in refusing the challenge of commoners, and would not dream of issuing one to such lesser beings. But a challenge from a fellow nobleman could not be honourably declined, even when duelling was forbidden by law and a victor who killed his opponent could be prosecuted for murder. From the 17th century onwards, governments made vigorous efforts to suppress duelling by severe and exemplary punishments, but these laws continued to be defied. As one 16th-century Frenchman put it: 'Our lives and our goods are the king's. Our souls are God's, and honour is ours. For over my honour, my king is powerless.'

Honour, in fact, was a licence to defy the king and to flout his laws in circumstances of which the nobleman himself was the sole judge. As Montesquieu noted two centuries later, 'Honour has its own laws and rules, and cannot bend . . . it depends on its own caprice' and was 'less what one owes to others, than what one owes to oneself'. Accordingly, aristocratic life was strewn with quarrels about precedence – who walked first, who sat higher or sat rather than stood, who acknowledged whom, and with what words and gestures. 'The Nobility of this place', wrote the daughter of an English peer from Regensburg, the capital of the Holy Roman Empire, in 1716,

> might pass their time agreeably enough if they were less delicate on the point of Ceremony; but instead of joining in the design of making the Town as pleasant to one another as they can and improving their little Societys, they amuse themselves no other way than with perpetual Quarrels, which they take care to eternize by leaving them to their Successors . . . I think it very prudent to remain Neuter, tho' if I was to stay amongst them there would be no possibility of remaining so, their Quarrels running so high they will not be civil to those that visit their Adversarys.

These disputes seem amazingly trivial to modern perceptions, and often led to ridiculous and undignified jockeying, but nobles saw them as fundamental to their idea of themselves. Though himself a baron of old stock, Montesquieu was prepared to admit that in the end honour was nothing more than a prejudice. Yet he argued that by pandering to it, kings could induce noblemen to 'undertake all manner of difficult acts, needing determination, with no other reward than the fame of the actions'. Honour for Montesquieu, indeed, was the very mainspring of monarchies, which worked through kings rewarding nobles with recognition or rewards, also called 'honours', for their services. The motivations of honour might be private, but it must be publicly displayed for others to see. And the legacy of chivalry dictated that, however fearless or violent they were in legitimate combat, men of honour should be polite and restrained in everyday life, keep their word, seek always to deal justly, offer protection to the weak, and observe the requirements of religious piety. Men of honour, in fact, were also men of virtue. As a noble quality, virtue was as nebulous and hard to define as honour itself, and in many ways the two were contradictory. Virtue normally implied some sort of selflessness, whereas honour was all about self-glorification. But many theorists argued that good lineage meant nothing if those enjoying it were not also virtuous.

The code of chivalry also dictated that women should be treated with special respect – or at least women of appropriate rank. The infamous *droit de seigneur*, the right of a lord to sleep with a vassal's wife on the first night of his marriage, may scarcely ever have existed except in the prurient imagination of legend, but men of power often thought little of debauching helpless servant girls. And if as a last resort they were willing to marry rich commoner heiresses in order to restore shrunken fortunes, the preference of nobles was always for wives from their own social level. There respect often ended, and few eyebrows were raised when married noblemen took mistresses. When kings set the fashion, as they so often did, nobles felt no shame in following the royal example. But the honour of noble spouses, as of queens, was a different matter. Their main function was to give birth to legitimate heirs, and if they dared to sleep with men other than their husbands, it would usually be after this duty had been safely fulfilled. In chivalric tradition, the ultimate shame and betrayal, after cowardice, was to seduce the wife of one's lord. Even in extra-marital affairs, men and women of noble birth found it safer to consort with equals.

Service

The legal obligation of vassals to serve their lord in arms was in full decline in the kingdoms of Western Europe from the 13th century onwards. By contrast, in Russia the demands of service to the ruler steadily grew down to 1762. They were regarded as little more than slavery by the nobles of Russia's nearest western neighbour, the Polish-Lithuanian commonwealth. There, the *Szlachta* exulted in their 'golden freedom' not to serve. In practice, however, although their primary loyalty was to the commonwealth rather than to the king whom they elected, they were as ready to take up arms as nobles anywhere, imbued with the universal conviction that their ultimate function was to serve the community by defending it with their lifeblood. The history of many states before relatively modern times is made up of repeated clashes between kings and rebellious nobles. Some of the founding documents of political freedom, such as Magna Carta wrung out of King John in 1215 by Anglo-Norman barons, were the result of noble resistance to royal encroachment on their traditional entitlements. It is true that most produced no such lofty outcomes, but it is too easy to see aristocratic rebelliousness as selfish and irresponsible. What noble rebels most often wanted was the preservation of ways in which they saw themselves serving under the king. In those circumstances, revolt might appear a positive duty – a defence, indeed, of honour.

Even after the waning of feudalism, Western nobles expected to be given the opportunity to fight under warlike monarchs. Peaceable kings were regarded as unsatisfactory. With the eclipse of armoured knights and fortified castles in late medieval warfare, it became harder to find a role for ordinary nobles except as auxiliary cavalry, whose effectiveness was doubtful and deployment often suicidal in the face of massed pikes and guns wielded by trained mercenaries. But the advent of standing armies from the 17th century onwards brought a growing need for officers at every level and in every military branch. Newly established overseas empires also began to offer opportunities to younger and poorer siblings to win military renown. By the late 18th century, all respectable states had permanent military establishments in which noblemen dominated the upper ranks. Only the huge armies through which Napoleon overawed Europe were led largely by men of common origin, and even then not exclusively. A nobleman himself, Napoleon increasingly sought officers among the 'great names' of the old nobility whose family traditions had bred the habit of command. His ultimate defeat by noble-officered armies appeared to vindicate the age-old claims that military service was the outstanding way in which aristocrats served states. Only in the European wars of the 20th century did this sustaining myth begin to disintegrate.

A major source of discontent for aristocrats down the centuries has been that rulers were failing to consult them. Giving advice was seen as another essential way of serving. Most noblemen, of course, could never aspire to the ear of kings, but magnates regarded giving counsel both as a right and a duty. During royal minorities, great nobles expected power itself to be entrusted to them, collectively, although quarrels of precedence frequently marred their effectiveness. But it was a recurrent grievance against mature monarchs that they chose to be advised by low-born ministers or favourites rather than their 'natural' counsellors. Men of power in their own right, with extensive networks of clients to maintain and reward, they obviously had every interest in bolstering their own authority through access to the sovereign. They thought he owed them the right to serve him, rather than rely on those they saw as upstarts who, like the Cecils in Elizabethan and Jacobean England, or the Le Telliers or Colberts in Louis XIV's France, might go on to establish rival networks and dynasties.

These families had risen through another form of service, whose equivalence to military prowess only began to be asserted in the 16th century. Their founders were bureaucrats, educated men dedicated to operating the rapidly expanding apparatus of early modern states. They might manage the logistics of warfare and its heavy fiscal and financial consequences, but they did not themselves take to the field. Many established themselves in royal service by buying offices. In France, the ennobled higher echelons of the steadily expanding system of venality were coming to be known by the early 17th century as nobility of the robe, in contrast to the more traditional nobility of the sword. Most robe nobles served as judges in the royal courts, and soon enough their families were inter-marrying with aristocrats of the older service tradition. Many noble dynasties served successive monarchs down the generations, until hereditary venal offices were abolished in 1789. By then, the upper ranks of the judiciary and administration of most European states were staffed by noblemen who saw it as a profession. But the gentry who administered the localities in the

British Isles as justices of the peace would have repudiated any suggestion that they were civil servants. Unlike paid functionaries, they gave their service free, content solely with the recognition of social consequence which appointment to the bench implied.

Aristocrats have seldom felt the need to demonstrate in advance their fitness to serve. Before the 19th century, officers and officials were recruited not by formal and open competition but by nepotism. Objective procedures for assessing suitability were inconceivable, the only proof of merit or ability was in performance, and even when they proved manifestly lacking, it was seldom possible to get rid of noblemen once in place. It was therefore scarcely surprising that opportunities to serve largely came through powerful patrons, who preferred to recommend relatives, or people they knew, or to whom they owed favours. Great magnates would often have extensive bands of clients, 'affinities' or 'interests' made up of expectant retainers, whose prospects were their lords' as much as their own. Lords in turn attracted such followings by proven ability to gratify their ambitions. In the 15th and 16th centuries, magnates in the West supported their claims with virtual private armies of retainers – what some historians have called 'bastard feudalism'. Further east, such retinues persisted for another century, but sooner or later kings established a monopoly of legitimate force. Nevertheless, patronage networks remained the key to power in church and state until the advent of public examinations in the 19th century, and so long as they lasted noblemen were the main beneficiaries.

The irony was that nobles had always enjoyed a reputation for idleness. This was natural enough given their determination not to soil their hands with manual toil, their disdain for industrious or commercial activity, and their preference for ostentatious leisure. But nobles were generally eager for lives of honourable activity. Most aristocratic idleness was enforced, the unavoidable result of penury which put the costs of service beyond the pockets of petty gentry. Given the means, aristocrats usually took every opportunity to show that the superiority of their birth was reinforced by other qualities of value to the whole community. They also knew, of course, that successful service opened the way to material rewards. But whatever the motivation, aristocrats and their energies were the mainspring of pre-industrial states, and none – apart perhaps from the commercial Dutch Republic – could have functioned without them. Only in the course of the 19th century was their grip on power and its instruments eroded as fewer and fewer of their claims to natural superiority came to appear self-evident.

Chapter 3
Living nobly

The phrase is not old. It appears first to have been used by the French Duke de Lévis in 1808, when 20 years of tribulation for aristocrats seemed about to end with the creation of a new titled hierarchy by Napoleon. *Noblesse oblige*, he said: nobility has its obligations. Aristocrats were prevented by law from doing some things, and by beliefs about themselves from doing others. Since the waning of feudalism, not many laws have imposed more positive obligations, but everybody knew that true nobles were expected to behave in ways which reinforced their claims to social distinction and power, to 'live nobly'.

Land

Aristocracies are essentially pre-industrial elites. Historically, their power has been based on controlling or dominating the main economic resource of almost all societies before the 19th century: land. In Hungary, the very term for a noblemen meant 'well-possessioned'. Even in city republics created and enriched by trade, such as Venice or Genoa, members of the ruling castes were eventually expected to use their wealth to acquire landed estates. Only in the Dutch Republic did the commercial 'Regents' of the cities remain largely aloof from emulating the relatively poor landed nobility of the inland provinces.

Land conferred freedom from gainful employment. The ideal of landed income is to free its beneficiaries to do other things. The objective of the feudal bond was to allow mounted warriors to serve their lords instead of earning a living. Granted fiefs by lords in return for knight service, feudal vassals would subinfeudate their holdings in return for service or dues from the peasantry. And while in the West over the early modern centuries feudal tenures were gradually supplanted or overlaid by outright ownership or contractual leases, nobles continued to prefer rental to direct exploitation of their estates. Direct farming was seen not only as a distraction from more important things, but also as perilously close to seeking commercial gain. This did not mean that nobles were indifferent to the profits to be derived from landownership. Despite legends of aristocratic improvidence and heedless neglect of assets, most evidence suggests that nobles were careful, not to say greedy, managers of their wealth. But this care normally took the form of maximizing traditional rentals rather than intervening to promote investment in long-term productivity. In Eastern Europe, meanwhile, over the same period a captive labour force was created through the enserfment of a formerly free peasantry, which sustained the idleness of nobles long after military service ceased to be a formal obligation. Some nobles had always exploited their lands directly for profit, especially where estates were small. Among the Prussian *Junkers*, or the teeming nobilities of Poland or Hungary, smallholders would farm for the market, selling their grain or distilling it into spirits, ploughing the fields with wooden swords at their side to signify their status. But this was from necessity, not preference. The predominant noble ideal was landed holdings extensive enough to be cultivated by tenants or serfs, paying rents, dues, or labour services to their lord or his agent at a castle or manor house impressive enough to reflect the wealth of ownership and the prestige of lordship. Rich men everywhere with ambitions to achieve ennoblement knew that, sooner or later, they must invest their wealth in land and the lifestyle that went with it.

Only the poorest nobles, however, spent most of their time in the country. Living on rents freed their richer brethren from the day-to-day supervision of their estates, and in any case the landholdings of the richest were often widely scattered. Absenteeism, often scorned by historians as a sign of aristocratic indifference to the sources of wealth, was unavoidable for anyone with estates and seats in several provinces or principalities. Few nobles of means, in any case, could resist the social and fashionable attractions of town life. Aristocratic families in Spain or Italy notoriously visited their rural properties only infrequently, and in fine weather. Public officials, whether soldiers, magistrates, or bureaucrats, had duties which took them far from the land for long periods. One cause of widespread serf uprisings during the first decade of Catherine the Great's rule in Russia was the reappearance in the countryside of nobles freed of compulsory service in 1762 and now determined to exploit their serfs more systematically: clearly, in some cases, absenteeism could be positively benign. But the political importance of greater lords dictated that they should spend much of their time in courts and capitals, however grand the country houses they built or embellished to flaunt their authority in the countryside which provided their basic income.

Nor was agriculture the only source of landed revenues. Around expanding cities, landlords could build over their fields and grant leases for colossal sums. It made the fortunes of British ducal houses like the Bedfords and Westminsters, who cashed in on the westward growth of London. Similarly lucrative, in remoter districts, were mineral deposits, especially when early industrialization produced a surge in demand. Coal-mining brought untold wealth to the Duke de Croÿ in 18th-century France, or the Duke of Bridgewater in England. Selling his coal in nearby Manchester led Bridgewater into canal-building. In the next century, exporting coal through the port which the Marquess of Bute created at Cardiff helped to make him the richest man in Great Britain. Over much of the Continent, on the other hand, the fact that subsoil remained royal domain inhibited noble attempts to exploit the chance of owning mineral-rich lands.

Yet in aristocratic eyes, land has never been simply a source of income. Land also implied lordship, long after the feudal bond within which these terms originated had frayed. Substantial landowners dominated the society of their districts, and exercised residual feudal rights as lords of manors, with their own courts to enforce them. They made much of the benevolence and protection which they offered to their forelock-tugging tenantry – although for every instance of almshouses founded and vassals entertained, examples could be found of whole villages moved to make way for parkland, fields devastated by huntsmen, or dues and services extracted to the last letter or beyond. But, whether open-handed or rapacious, all these cases would demonstrate the unchallengeable authority that went with landownership down to the last decades of the 19th century, and often some way beyond.

Leisure

Aristocrats prize leisure. Classical education taught them to revere the Roman noble ideal of ease, *otium* – as opposed to *negotium*, which meant trouble, difficulty, or simply business. Leisure was an essential prerequisite for aristocrats to do everything else expected of them. This included ways of entertaining themselves, many of which echoed more serious noble pursuits.

Killing has always been a preferred way for gentlemen to pass the time. When not at war, knights still risked their lives in jousting. Fencing was also deemed a quintessential noble accomplishment until far into the 19th century, sustaining the defence of honour in duels. When portable firearms became practical, shooting became another gentlemanly hallmark, useful itself in duels but mainly deployed against birds and animals – vermin to farmers, but increasingly bred or allowed to breed simply for gentlemen to shoot them. Above all, there was hunting, the perfect training for mounted warfare, but also honing riding skills in ages when no mode of transport was faster than a horse. All gentlemen could ride, and their prestige was reflected in the quality of their mounts. When the Protestant Irish parliament wished in the 18th century to destroy the authority of Catholic gentry, they forbade any Catholic to possess a horse worth more than five pounds. Deer were the main quarry of huntsmen, along with wolves in earlier times and foxes more recently, when more serious beasts had been hunted to extinction. Astonishing passions were poured into hunting, and richer lords kept large stables and carefully nurtured packs of hounds. And while extensive forests were set aside largely for their convenience, in the heat of the chase they thought nothing of rampaging through cultivated fields or of the damage they might do to other property. For the socially ambitious, riding to hounds was an important way of integration into aristocratic society.

Horses could also be raced, and in aristocratic culture bloodstock was almost as important as blood sports. Richer noblemen bred racehorses, and race meetings became important places for social intercourse and even the transaction of public affairs. The Jockey Clubs which continue to govern racing remain one of the last redoubts of aristocratic exclusivism. Nobles rarely competed themselves, except for petty gentry in local events, but they led the way in betting on the results. Gambling appealed to every aristocratic instinct – the courage, the risk, the grand gesture, the glory of effortless success, stoical indifference to loss. Nor was it confined to the racecourse. Over early modern times, the boredom of long evenings in draughty mansions made 'play' at cards a universal pastime, and at the highest level huge sums were wagered. Anecdotes abound of fortunes and patrimonies lost on the turn of a card, payment made as a matter of honour. As so often, such high-profile cases were more spectacular than typical. Whole nobilities would have been ruined if they had not been.

They were simply periodic warnings of where immoderate pursuit of fashionable pastimes might lead.

Whereas hunting and shooting were largely the preserve of men, cards were played with equal enthusiasm by women. Also shared equally was aristocratic taste for the theatre. Theatricals were an established part of elite education for both sexes from the late 16th century onwards, and public theatres from their origins around the same time were regarded as places where the fashionable came to see each other as much as the performance. When nobility was ostracized by the French revolutionaries, the Parisian theatre was brought to the brink of collapse. Until the late 18th century, most successful plays were about the doings and dilemmas of noble characters, and amateur theatricals, like those planned over so many of the pages of Jane Austen's *Mansfield Park* as an alternative to endless cards, were popular among the occupants of country houses throughout the 18th century. Dancing as an aristocratic accomplishment for both sexes had a much longer history, and women were increasingly expected to acquire at least rudimentary musical skills.

Many of the indoor accomplishments and amusements of aristocrats came together from the late 17th century at spas. The mineral waters of a small town in the bishopric of Liège gave this generic name to watering places with curative springs throughout Europe, and there fashionable society, not all of it ailing, tended to gather. Carlsbad or Baden-Baden in Germany, Bagnères or Plombières in France, and above all Bath in England, the largest spa in Europe by the later 18th century, became centres of high fashion which anyone with claims to notability felt obliged to frequent. Ensconced in elegant lodgings, the distinguished visitors enjoyed a constant round of polite sociability a world away from the rough pastimes of their (presumed) medieval ancestors. What they had in common was a shared determination to flaunt their rank.

Display

Aristocracy is ostentatious. Distinction needs to show itself and impress onlookers. The oldest noble badge of distinction, the coat of arms, began as a means of identification on the battlefield, but became an emblem to be emblazoned on every item of importance: buildings, coaches, servants' liveries, books, notepaper, signet rings, tombs. A whole arcane science of heraldry grew up around it. Nobles also prized elaborate names, and sometimes improbable ways of pronouncing them to confuse unwary inferiors: Cholmondeley, Broglie, Castries. Less definably, aristocrats have always sought to dress distinctively, aware that Roman senators had worn special togas and footwear. In the 15th and 16th centuries, sumptuary laws in several states attempted to prevent commoners from wearing the rich garments thought fitting for noblemen – but too many wealthy commoners could afford them, and too many nobles could not. Nobles who had the means simply continued to seek ways of looking different – whether obviously, by always wearing swords, orders or decorations, jewels, or more subtly by choice of cloth or cut. In France, the red heels fashionable at Louis XIV's court were a synonym for nobility for generations after the vogue had passed.

They always tried to avoid travelling on foot. The elevation and speed, not to mention the cost, of a horse was a powerful physical manifestation of rank. Over the early modern centuries, carriages proliferated, with attendant grooms, postillions, and running footmen alongside, all serving, as John Ruskin piquantly observed, for 'the abashing of plebeian beholders'. Servants of all types, in fact, were an essential accompaniment, and the greater the noble, the more numerous his retinue was expected to be. Magnates with far-flung estates had to maintain staff on all of them, if only for the upkeep of the castles or great houses which were the most important of all manifestations of aristocratic power and authority.

6. George Villiers, Duke of Buckingham (1592–1628): a royal favourite raised 'from the dust' displays his Order of the Garter

If country squires were forced by penury to pass Spartan lives in crumbling manor houses or castles whose military value had been eliminated with the invention of gunpowder, building or improving a fitting residence was a constant priority for aristocrats with money to spare or good credit. Magnates would maintain urban palaces in capital cities, such as those still to be found scattered throughout Paris, Vienna, Prague, or St. Petersburg. In London, only Spencer House still evokes the memory of great houses now gone like those of the Dukes of Devonshire or Northumberland. But the true palaces of these peers were, and are, in the country, at Althorp, Chatsworth, and Alnwick. Unfortified country houses made their first substantial appearance in an England unthreatened by warfare in the 16th century. Many were built on the ruins of dissolved monasteries. By the 18th century, they, and the parks surrounding them, were being imitated all over the Continent. The greatest seats, such as the Prince de Condé's Chantilly in France, the Prince de Ligne's Beloeil in Belgium, or, most famous of all, the Esterházy palaces in Austria and Hungary where Haydn was retained as resident composer, can still be visited. Country house building, ever more grandiose, went on until the crisis of agricultural revenues in the last decades of the 19th century, even though it was widely acknowledged that building was the surest way to dissipate a fortune. In the world of aristocratic show, however, always obsessed too with fashion, few were content to continue living in gloomy fortresses, especially when rich newcomers were constantly announcing their arrival by constructing houses in the latest style. Only in the 20th century did 'stately homes' come to be viewed by many of their owners as a liability. By the time, with the return of post-Second World War prosperity, they had come to be widely regarded as a precious cultural heritage, many had been demolished or converted into institutions.

It is scarcely a coincidence that so many of these residences look theatrical. They constitute an essential stage, or backdrop, for the theatre of aristocratic show. At the heart of great estates, nobles

7. Esterházy Palace, Hungary: one of several country seats where Haydn was retained as *Kappelmeister*

could entertain in them and demonstrate the oldest values associated with aristocracy: generosity and hospitality. Great houses were often open to the public on request, centuries before they were opened to paying visitors. Tenants could be periodically entertained with food, drink, games, and spectacles, even if this was only the sight of hounds moving off for the hunt. All nobles considered it a supreme honour to entertain their monarch – although rulers sometimes used royal progresses deliberately to deplenish the wealth of over-mighty subjects called upon to put up their entire court. Louis XIV, notoriously, was so appalled by the opulence deployed to welcome him in 1661 by his superintendent of finances, Fouquet, that he had him arrested and imprisoned for life. And finally, there was the spectacle of death. Nobles favoured pompous and elaborate funerals, and expected burial inside parish churches alongside their ancestors, if not in family mausolea. They knew that those surviving them would commemorate them with elaborate monuments and wordy inscriptions setting out their virtues and achievements, carefully adding their contribution to the ever-lengthening record of family distinction.

Display is expensive. Even the wealthiest aristocrats have tended to spend up to the limits of their income, and often beyond. A powerful literary stereotype has always been that of the improvident nobleman weighed down with debts heedlessly incurred and repaid scandalously in arrears, if at all. It is true that the only casual debts which nobles paid punctiliously were gambling ones, involving honour. Tradesmen and contractors, by contrast, could often be kept waiting for years, and in England until the mid-19th century, peers could not be imprisoned for debt. Thousands of creditors risked ruin when occasionally a great nobleman went spectacularly bankrupt. But, with the line between bankruptcy and fraud far less clear than it later became, the dishonour scandalized fellow nobles. Yet selling property to stave off debt was not always easy. The most extensive estates were often secured by tightly drafted entails. Governments, in any case, were usually reluctant to see the decimation of noble landholdings by forced sales, and in the later 18th century several East European rulers set up land banks to lend petty nobles a financial lifeline at advantageous rates. Established to keep noble wealth intact, they seldom foreclosed if borrowers defaulted. When estates were entailed, foreclosure was in any case legally impossible. Yet the most extensive noble mortgages were seldom taken out to fund frivolity, but to ease the burden of dowries and family settlements, not to mention improving or extending estates. Such borrowings were carefully planned and budgeted for, the very opposite of imprudent. Myths of heedless open-handedness, much treasured by critics of nobility, were often carefully fostered by nobles themselves. But if they really had been so careless with their money, few nobilities would have survived for very long.

Education

Effortless achievement, or at least the appearance of it, was a
treasured aspect of noble display. Superiority ought to be
self-evident. The supreme quality of the polished characters in
Baldassare Castiglione's *The Courtier* (1528), perhaps the most
studied of many manuals of aristocratic conduct, was *sprezzatura*,
scorn for any appearance of effort. Medieval nobilities placed little
value on formal education. The only training they required was to
equip them for success on the battlefield, and even here the
assumption of innate courage outshone the need for learning the
soldier's trade. It was among the unmilitary urban patriciates of
northern Italy, modelling themselves on the elites of ancient Rome
but employing mercenaries to do their fighting, that cultivation of
literature and the arts began to re-establish itself as aristocratic. It
was slow to spread, even among the fashion-conscious French.
Castiglione's sophisticated courtiers were constantly lamenting
that all French noblemen cared about was arms. A hundred years
later, French prejudice against learning was still strong.
Government was no business, mused Cardinal Richelieu, for men
'more loaded with Latin than with lands'. But by then, Latin had
become one of the mainstays of education even for the landed.
States of expanding ambition needed literate laymen to manage
their administration, and rewards at the highest level were too
great for nobles to resist. The religious splits of the Reformation
also made all confessions anxious to imbue the leaders of society
with a closer understanding of what they were supposed to believe.
With this in mind, the Jesuits, founded by a noble Spanish soldier
of fortune, made it their business to become the educators of most
of the Catholic elites of Europe and its overseas outposts. The 16th
century saw a spectacular expansion in institutions of superior
education throughout Europe, and by its end, nobles were widely
expected to be not only literate but also Latinate. Still only a
minority attended university, and fewer still took degrees involving
the possibility of examination (however perfunctory) by social

inferiors, but steadily increasing numbers studied at colleges and academies where some traditional aristocratic accomplishments such as riding or fencing were taught alongside letters.

The sheer expense of such an education excluded all but the richest and most ambitious commoners from attempting to share in it. In medieval times, sons from the upper ranks learned aristocratic ways as pages in the households of princes or magnates, and this practice continued in certain circles. Private tutors were also widely employed to impart a distinctively aristocratic education, and they would accompany their charges on what by the 17th and 18th centuries would come to be seen as the culmination of any wealthy young gentleman's formation: the Grand Tour. Lasting from a few months to several years, the Tour was designed to enable young men destined for public careers to get to know the world of high culture and high society at first hand. On it, they were meant to frequent courts, observe military exercises, perfect foreign languages, inspect monuments, and acquire cultural souvenirs. They would all aim to end up in Italy, the land of art, music, and the classics. They would certainly visit France, too, and perhaps Holland. But the hope was that everywhere they would, as the Earl of Chesterfield advised his son in 1748, 'imitate ... with discernment and judgement, the real perfections of the good company into which you may get; copy their politeness, their carriage, their address, and the easy and well-bred turn of their conversation.'

Yet a Grand Tour was always beyond the pockets of most nobles, and even among the richest the tradition barely survived the upheavals of the revolutionary and Napoleonic wars. Eventually, governments became worried by the cost of educating young noblemen up to the level of their status and traditional vocation. Over the 18th century, military academies were established to offer scholarships and officer training to poorer nobles. It was in such establishments that the young Napoleon Bonaparte, from an old but threadbare Corsican family, learned the rudiments of soldiering. The great wars he fought demonstrated the increasing importance of military professionalism, and by the mid-19th century, all great powers had central officer schools whose cadets were overwhelmingly noble. But before entering them, they still preferred to be educated apart, alongside their own kind. In most countries, a handful of elite schools, such as Eton or Westminster in England, or the great left-bank colleges of Paris, took in disproportionate noble numbers. The Russian Alexander Lycée, founded in 1811, only accepted nobles. A core curriculum of classics gave all who underwent it a private language and range of reference for life, while often brutal discipline and (in the 19th century) frenzied promotion of sports and games were thought a good preparation for lives of authority and action. Perhaps a majority of nobles continued to mistrust too much 'book learning' as beyond the requirements of a gentleman; but all felt obliged, after the French Revolution challenged the whole rationale of aristocracy, to prepare themselves more systematically to confront the modern world.

Or at least men did. For aristocratic women, educational requirements evolved hardly at all. As with men, it was thought desirable, if not more so, that they should be educated apart. Girls of the highest rank, destined from birth to make strategic dynastic marriages, were privately tutored or, in Catholic countries, placed in the care of aristocratic nuns in exclusive convents. Ladies of the highest cultural accomplishments were always present in high society, from those fictionally guiding the discussion in Castiglione's *Courtier*, to the great *salon* hostesses who did so much to promote the values of the Enlightenment in the France of Louis XV. But even as polished an adviser as Chesterfield thought that no woman needed to know Latin, and to a provincial like Napoleon women were little more than 'machines to make children'. They needed to be polite, but submissive; numerate, for keeping household accounts; able to dance, and preferably to sing and play a stringed instrument (blowing was deemed inelegant). If they rode, it could only be side-saddle. But in the end, they knew

53

that their only essential function as aristocrats was to be, as one 21st-century English duchess put it, 'brood mares'.

Courts and courtiers

For centuries, the conventional image of the aristocrat, the ideal type, was that of the courtier. In the torrent of denunciation which surrounded the French revolutionary attack on nobility, most of the habits and pretensions ascribed to nobles in general were those associated with the court: haughty disdain for and indifference to inferiors, servility to those above, hypocrisy, greed, extravagance, debts, nepotism, and the whole range of moral depravity. A long literary tradition underlay these charges, much of it lovingly honed by envious fellow nobles unable to afford the expense of court life, and observing it sourly from the provinces. It was ironic that they all ended up tarred with the same brush. Yet courts did set an ideal standard until far into the 19th century. 'The language, the air, the dress, and the manners of the Court,' Chesterfield warned his son, 'are the only true standard ... for a man of parts, who has been bred at Court, and used to keep the best company, will distinguish himself, and is to be known from the vulgar, by every word, attitude, gesture, and even look.'

The attractions of courts were power, prestige, and remuneration – all closely interlinked. Courts were the 'households' of monarchs, who, in addition to the power which they wielded and dispensed, gloried in being the first gentlemen of their kingdoms, the undisputed senior noblemen, setting standards of display and aristocratic conduct imitated, according to means, throughout the noble hierarchy. The confidence of kings was the key to power, and they gave it only to men they knew. Great nobles, in turn, felt entitled to that confidence, but to earn it, they needed access to the ruler, to be seen in his company, share his pleasures and diversions, win his attention. Courts were never the exclusive preserve of noblemen. They were the nucleus of vast networks of functions and services managed largely by commoners. But only nobles felt entitled to be there, and it was such a magnet that some of them even needed to be kept away. The system of 'honours of the court' instituted by Louis XV of France (1715–74), which excluded any family not noble since 1400 from presentation to the king or hunting with him, originated less as a sop to genealogical pride than a logistic device to hold numbers down.

Yet many qualifying families did not stay after their presentation conferred a ritual recognition. The true qualification for being at court was being able to afford it. A constant round of fashion, lavish entertainments, polite gambling, not to mention the need to follow the monarch on progresses, was ruinously expensive. Most courtier families also felt the need to keep separate town houses in capital cities, places with expensive and fashionable attractions of their own. Even the greatest incomes were strained by such demands, and one of the constant preoccupations of courtiers was to supplement them by handouts to which only they had access – pensions, offices, and well-paid sinecures from the king's revenues. At this level, the less they could afford to be at court, the more they needed to be there.

And in absolute monarchies, which most states more-or-less were until the 19th century, court was the forum of high politics, the location of all the levers of power, a place of protection, promotion, and patronage. Even in Great Britain, a parliamentary state from the later 17th century, the prestige of sharing the royal presence, and the ceremonial and material rewards of doing so, could be substantial, at least until the widowhood of Queen Victoria. Few ministers until her reign could hope to hold a secure parliamentary majority for long without the monarch's overt support. When he made himself an emperor, Napoleon felt the need to uphold his new dignity by resurrecting something like the court which the French Revolution had destroyed. His downfall made successor states reluctant to emulate him, and the 19th century saw the size and political role of courts shrink away. Their role as centres of fashion followed: eventually, indeed, they came to represent everything that was positively old-fashioned. But these shrivelled relics of once-glittering theatres of power were still seats of supreme hereditary authority, and in them the monopolistic role of aristocrats of old stock was more clearly established than ever. Until well into the 20th century in Great Britain, the peak of the metropolitan social season was when young ladies from good families established their credentials by formal presentation to the monarch as beginners in the life of high society – or, in the language of old Versailles, *débutantes*.

Diversity

For all their role in setting standards, only a small minority of nobles ever went near a court. Many positively hated courtiers as greedy, unfairly fortunate parasites. Courtiers in turn despised and ridiculed the rustic or bourgeois manners of such onlookers. This antagonism, called in 17th-century England 'court versus country', was only one of innumerable rifts among aristocrats in every country, and at every level. The inequality fundamental to any idea of nobility did as much to divide nobles from one another as from the majority of the population.

Nobility is a tissue of minute differences lovingly treasured, each one affording grounds for a sense of superiority or inferiority. Court/country antagonisms were obviously a particular manifestation of discrepancies in wealth. But new nobles, invariably well-off, were disdained by courtiers and petty squires alike for their lack of ancestors. Every family tree offered countless ways for nobles to measure themselves against one another. Antagonisms could also be professional. Military men seldom had much time for pen-pushing administrators or judges whose professions required no courage and brought no glory yet who held the fate of armies or litigants in their hands. Titled families routinely scorned those with none, and the promise of promotion within the titular hierarchy was one of a monarch's most potent inducements. Considerations of this sort all came into play when families contemplated marriage alliances: nobody wished to marry beneath themselves, yet they were almost always prepared to overlook any perceived disparities between possible partners if one side offered overwhelming advantages in prestige or, most often, wealth. Even the oldest, most elevated, not to say opulent, families would swallow their pride at the prospect of heiresses of inferior status but richer than themselves.

Nor have any two nobilities of different countries ever been alike in every feature. Poland, Hungary, and Spain teemed with petty nobles, most of them inevitably not wealthy. In certain north Spanish provinces, every male was deemed a *hidalgo*, the son of a distinguished father. In the British Isles, by contrast, only peers have ever been legally noble. Inevitably, there were wide disparities in the proportion of the population represented by groups so variously defined, but only in countries where nobility was widely defined, like Poland or parts of Spain, did the proportion ever much exceed 1–2%, diminishing in later times when overall populations expanded. Moreover, however pervasive the ideal of living off landed income, landless nobles were constantly being spawned by the operation of inheritance laws which either produced morcellation of patrimonies or disproportionately favoured the eldest son. Some landless nobles found reputable employment as soldiers, but many more were forced into occupations normally spurned in aristocratic circles – including trade, both wholesale and retail. Even nobles able to remain appropriately landed extracted the surplus generated by their tenants in a wide variety of ways: in Western Europe, increasingly by cash rents, supplemented to differing extents by residual feudal dues and services from vassals; and east of the Elbe from the forced labour of serfs tied to the land or (in Russia) owned personally.

And the power which nobles wielded in their communities was nowhere the same. In city republics like Venice or Genoa, the entire nobility enjoyed collective power. The *Szlachta* of pre-partition Poland saw themselves as a complete nation, and

8. A great Polish magnate, Count Stanislas Potocki, depicted by
Jacques-Louis David, 1781

elected representatives to govern them at every level, right up to the king himself. The British parliament was likewise largely controlled by aristocratic interests until the later 19th century, and their blocking power in the House of Lords was only definitively vanquished in 1911. Wherever else parliamentary institutions existed before the 19th century, whether national or provincial, nobilities normally had a house to themselves, but nowhere were their precise powers identical. Nobilities who enjoyed an autonomy they called freedom pitied the subservience of counterparts compelled to live under absolute monarchs. These rulers would routinely label any show of noble independence as rebellion, or republicanism. They all lived in dread of overmighty subjects. Yet none of them ever dreamed of trying to govern without the collaboration at every level of noblemen, and if they chose ministers low in rank, they showered them with new titles and rewards so that they could look any other subject in the face. But even under absolute monarchs, the day-to-day autonomy of nobles varied widely, depending on the size of the kingdom, the differing constitutions of realms assembled often by dynastic accident or chance conquest, and the strength of traditions of service and loyalty.

The broad outlines of what aristocracy was or is, and how aristocrats behave, seem to dissolve into a blur when tested against the sheer variety of examples and exceptions. Nobles themselves were not deceived. They could recognize their own when they saw them, however different. So could the rest of society, which, accepting their hegemony in every sphere of life, was profoundly influenced by their values and example. In some ways, it still is.

Chapter 4
Impacts and legacies

As power elites, and even as residual fragments dusted with the dim memory of former power, aristocracies have always commanded deference. They have expected their superiority to be overtly acknowledged by others. In earlier times in the West, and until much later in Eastern European lands of serfdom, nobles would not hesitate to punish lack of respect with violence. As late as 1725, the Chevalier de Rohan had Voltaire beaten up in a Paris street for an impertinent remark. Fifty years later, an Englishman travelling in Ireland noted that nothing satisfied an Irish landlord but 'unlimited submission. Disrespect or anything tending towards sauciness he may punish with his cane or horsewhip with the most perfect security: a poor man would have his bones broken if he offered to lift his hand in his own defence.' By this time, English sensibilities were shocked by such behaviour, but English aristocrats still expected demonstrative deference from their social inferiors. A decade still later, the French revolutionaries would turn deference on its head, making 'aristocracy' a term of political abuse, and turn nobles briefly into pariahs. Everywhere outside France, nobles were appalled and terrified. This spasm did not last, but the memory of it haunted them throughout the following century. Never again could deference be taken entirely for granted. Now there were always people prepared to denounce aristocracy without fear and, given the occasion, renew the attacks pioneered in revolutionary France.

Nevertheless, the deferential reflex survived. It could scarcely be otherwise in a continent where nobles, their ways and values, had dominated government and society for so long.

Dependencies

As rich conspicuous consumers, aristocrats in their heyday were always a major source of employment. No noble household, however modest, could function without servants, and the size of retinues was an important part of aristocratic display. In the 15th and 16th centuries, magnates travelled with outriders and lackeys running into hundreds, all in livery. And if in later centuries such ostentation came to seem vulgar, and in the eyes of suspicious kings even threatening, aristocratic tastes and pastimes could not be fully indulged without the support of valets, chambermaids, footmen, butlers, cooks, gardeners, foresters, gamekeepers, grooms, kennelmen, huntsmen, coachmen, porters, handymen. Greater houses might even employ librarians (like Thomas Hobbes at 17th-century Chatsworth) or musicians (like Josef Haydn, and an orchestra to play his works, at 18th-century Eisenstadt and Esterház). Few of the elaborate clothes favoured by aristocrats could be put on without the help of dressers; and for some pampered masters no service was too small. The father of Alexander Herzen, founder of Russian socialism, even had his daily newspapers warmed to protect the delicacy of his fingers. And where noblemen were concentrated, as at royal courts, the largest element of the population was made up of their servants: over 44,000 people lived at Versailles, a town with no business except the court, on the eve of the French Revolution.

Nor did the reach of the several hundred courtier families they served end there. Most of them also felt obliged to keep an establishment in the nearby capital. There, their demands sustained a massive range of luxury industries supplying their fashionable wants, from everyday foodstuffs to furniture, clothes, decorative items, and jewellery. Five representative courtier families recently studied gave business to 1,800 manufacturers and tradesmen throughout late 18th-century Paris. And the fashionable tentacles of the court stretched even further. When mourning was declared for deceased members of the royal family or foreign monarchs, the court donned black and the staple silk industry of Lyon went into temporary recession. Naturally, therefore, the outbreak of an anti-aristocratic revolution spelled economic disaster for the manufacturers and tradesmen of France's first and second cities. One of the many motives of Napoleon in setting up a glittering court of titled dignitaries was to restore the prosperity of the luxury trades. On the other hand, the grand French tradition of fine dining takes its origin from restaurants established by the unemployed cooks of great families brought low by revolutionary persecution.

On a smaller scale, provincial capitals, or the residential seats of petty German princelings, lived by the needs and appetites of local nobilities. Nobles have always been great litigants, and the economic rhythms of judicial centres were set by the annual arrival of gentry pursuing cases often going back generations. They might not bring the retinues or luxurious appetites of metropolitan magnates, but nobody doubted the wealth and animation that came with them. In pre-industrial times, too, nobles were the main patrons of large-scale construction, building or endlessly improving their country houses or the gardens and parks surrounding them, not to mention endowing amenities such as market halls or almshouses. Many of the most spectacular ecclesiastical buildings also went up as a result of aristocratic patronage, either direct or at one remove through the ambitions of noble prelates, abbots, or chapters.

The luxury of courts, capitals, and chapters, it is true, passed the majority of nobles by, exacerbating their hatred and suspicion of plutocratic metropolitan elites. Most made do with a handful of servants or a single factotum, and had little alternative to letting their castellated manor houses crumble around them. Theirs was a life, as one early 18th-century commentator (a French marquis living at the court of Berlin) described it, of 'hunting, hitting peasants, impregnating their farmers' daughters, going to law against their village priests for a few honorific rights, and getting drunk with their stewards on Sundays'. Nevertheless, they still expected deference from their neighbours, and if money unexpectedly came their way, their instinct was to spend on the same sort of vanities as their more opulent fellows.

Economic diversions

Whether the outlay of so much income on display was truly productive was one of the many questions raised in 1776 by Adam Smith in the *Wealth of Nations*. 'In those towns', he wrote,

> which are principally supported by the constant or occasional residence of a court, and in which the inferior ranks of people are chiefly maintained by the spending of revenue, they are in general idle, dissolute, and poor ... The idleness of the greater part of the people who are maintained by the expense of revenue, corrupts, it is probable, the industry of those who ought to be maintained by the employment of capital, and renders it less advantageous to employ a capital there than in other places.

There was also the influence of example. When the richest, most powerful, and most eye-catching members of society made a point of despising trade and industry as demeaning, nobody with dreams of social advancement was likely to embrace them with any enthusiasm, or to keep on with them a moment longer than they need. Most nobilities sustained their wealth and power by constantly siphoning off the resources of ambitious commoners, recruiting (if seldom explicitly welcoming) and incorporating into their ranks the most energetic and resourceful families of the commercial middle classes or bourgeoisie. It was prudent enough for rich men to sink some of their resources into the safest of all investments in a pre-industrial economy: land. But there was usually more to it than that. To buy land was to advertise social ambition, to join the landowners who dominated every aspect of life. In France, additionally, until 1789 huge sums were also invested in the purchase of ennobling offices. Land at least could be made economically productive, even if not as impressively as trade and industry, but offices were completely sterile. Many were also bought with borrowed money that might otherwise have been invested more adventurously. It is true that aristocratic dominion did not prevent the commercial and industrial breakthroughs that made Great Britain the first modern economy. An aristocratically dominated parliament, in fact, did much to authorize and create the commercial infrastructure which facilitated these advances. But what might well have kept more capital than elsewhere in the hands and enterprises of commoners was the difficulty of acquiring land in a market immobilized by rising rents, primogeniture, and entail. When they could, however – even when, in the 19th century, Great Britain was the 'workshop of the world' – successful British industrialists showed themselves as eager as ever to buy country estates, build or extend mansions, adopt the leisured lifestyle, and send their sons to public schools to learn to be true gentlemen and bury their commercial origins. Contempt for trade, science, and technology suffused public school education far into the 20th century – an important element, some historians claim, in British economic decline.

With so much land in aristocratic hands, the practice and development of agriculture could hardly be unaffected by their preferences and priorities. Maximizing rental for minimal outlay was the consistent aim of most landlords, and they were seldom prepared to forgo immediate revenue by reinvesting for long-term gains. Even when, as in 18th-century England, enclosure of common lands, long leases, security of tenure, and a high reinvestment rate underpinned spectacular rises in agricultural productivity, the example was lost on most Continental, or indeed Irish, landlords. Their preference was for short leases to the highest bidder, and indifference to the depredations of profiteering middlemen who sublet, exhausted the soil, and moved on. In Eastern Europe, the advantages of a captive serf labour force working unpaid were taken for granted, despite the clear inefficiencies which resulted both in terms of cultivating the lords' demesnes and the relative neglect of serfs' own holdings. The preachings of governments about the economic advantages of serf emancipation fell on deaf ears, and when rulers began to limit the demands which lords could make, they ran into fierce resistance and evasion. In maritime Europe, the attacks of abolitionists on colonial slavery met with a similar outraged response. There was extensive noble investment in British and French slavery, while the more prosperous slave traders and Caribbean planters often used their profits to buy into landed estates and the aristocratic lifestyle back in Europe.

Efficiency was never an aristocratic concern. When the French revolutionaries attempted to abolish nobility in 1790, they did so in the name of careers open to the talents, or what became known, a century and a half later, as meritocracy. Aristocrats were always quick to claim that merit was inseparable from their true nature. What they meant by merit, however, was not some objective quality, but success in behaving as aristocrats should. Merit in commoners meant doing the same. Advancement under the rule of aristocracy, however, depended not on ability but on influence, contacts, patronage, 'protection', or what in Great Britain was called 'interest'. The aristocratic way was nepotism, a preference for promoting and doing business with people like themselves, and best of all their own kin. However ruthlessly the priority of keeping family patrimonies together left younger scions penniless, a sense of family solidarity often impelled heads of families to procure employment for their junior members. Soliciting patronage was an important aristocratic activity at every level, and one measure of a noblemen's prestige was his ability to find places for relatives and clients in government, the church, or the armed forces. Defenders of the sale of offices actually argued that venality was a more just and more efficient way of securing state servants than such clientage. But so long as aristocrats ruled, those in power felt no incentive to find objective ways of identifying ability and aptitude. Their every instinct, after all, inclined them to believe that these qualities were most likely to be hereditary.

War

The warrior origins of aristocratic power, and the primacy always accorded in aristocratic ideology to martial courage and achievements, gave nobles a vested interest in warfare. In the Middle Ages, great magnates were invariably warlords, supporting their pretensions with private armies of retainers. Kings offended them at their peril, and during minorities or when rulers themselves lacked warlike qualities, baronial rivalries could plunge whole realms into civil war. In the religious wars of 16th-century France, observed Montaigne from the sidelines, the Duke de Guise encountered such implacable rivalry from the future Henry IV, then no more than an heir presumptive to the throne, that

> he had recourse to war, as to a last resort, that might defend the honour of his house...; the bitterness of these two characters was the principle of the war so enflamed today;...only the death of one or the other could bring it to an end...As to Religion...of which both make show, it is a fine pretext to make their own parties follow them, but its interest touches neither.

Noble soldiers of fortune, who drifted from one to another of the great conflicts of the next century, were equally indifferent to the causes for which they ostensibly fought. What mattered was the chance to behave as noblemen should, and the depredations of war for subject populations concerned them not at all. With so much of education and leisure devoted to riding, hunting, and fencing, it was natural that young nobles should dream of any opportunity to distinguish themselves on real battlefields. One of the recognized objectives of the German equivalent of the Grand Tour, the *Kavalierstour*, with which many young nobles rounded off their education in the 17th century, was to see, and if possible take part in, military action.

It is true that this was the century in which kings finally achieved a monopoly of permissible violence. Private armies were now becoming a thing of the past. Yet the establishment of royal standing armies with extensive bodies of officers gave nobles a new and expanding outlet for their warlike energies, and the dynastic origin of so many of the conflicts undertaken by kings was one which they could readily understand. For officers, a state of war meant full employment rather than half-pay. It meant activity and excitement rather than the boredom of garrison life. It also brought the only chance of accelerated promotion, and the opportunity to accumulate unexpected fortunes. And for the magnates who normally monopolized high command, war was the opportunity to immortalize themselves and add lustre to the annals of their families.

Nobilities therefore constituted a relentless, steady source of pressure pushing states towards resolving their differences on the battlefield. Noble pacifists have always been a relative rarity, and monarchs or ministers seeking to resolve differences peaceably, objects of contempt. When the French revolutionaries bade defiance to the whole of Europe, nobles everywhere clamoured to teach the upstarts a lesson. And, however lamentable the record of noble-led armies against meritocratic French generals over the next generation, their successive victories over Napoleon between 1812 and 1815 seemed a belated vindication of aristocratic leadership. Over the subsequent century, non-nobles penetrated the officer corps of the leading European nations in ever-increasing numbers, but the high commands remained firmly in aristocratic hands, as did policy-making in most governments. And it has been persuasively argued that a major impulse driving the powers to war in 1914 was the belief that this was the best way to preserve and reinforce the traditional hegemony of these threatened elites against the encroaching forces of liberalism, democracy, and modernism in general. It would, of course, be absurd to blame the inherent aggressiveness of states and societies on aristocrats alone. But over much of their history both their interests and their ideologies have predisposed them to use their power in support of organized violence.

Liberty

Although nobles have always expected deference and acceptance of the social hierarchy of which they were the summit, they have usually been much more ambivalent about supreme political authority. The dictates of honour acknowledged no higher law; and in medieval times kings were seen as little more than first among equals, scarcely more than the most successful among competing warlords. Aristocratic obedience to them was therefore seldom more than conditional. Baronial rebellion defied kings who claimed too much authority. Sometimes it culminated in their overthrow and replacement by a less assertive scion of the royal house. More often, a defeated monarch surrendered by accepting formal constraints on his power. The most celebrated was no doubt the Great Charter extracted by the English barons from King John in 1215, subsequently seen in all English-speaking countries (however fancifully) as the founding document of their freedoms. Seven years later, at the other end of Europe, the king of Hungary conceded a formal right of rebellion in the 'Golden Bull' of 1222, and down to 1791 the Polish *Szlachta* regarded as part of their own 'Golden Freedom' the right to resist any new law by forming armed 'confederations'. Such rights of resistance were the corollary of an even more fundamental freedom – the right to elect the monarch himself. The Holy Roman Emperor was always elected by a handful of German territorial electoral princes and archbishops. In Hungary, royal election disappeared in practice in the 16th century, and in law in the 17th; but in Poland by then, it was reinforced by the *pacta conventa*, a formal contract agreed by each king prior to his election, in which he normally promised to make no innovations. But everywhere monarchs at their coronations customarily swore to observe certain fundamental laws, and nobles were the only people powerful enough to hold them to their word. Nor did the deposition or assassination of kings deemed to have broken their oaths end with the Middle Ages. Noble conspirators complaining of tyranny murdered a king of Sweden in 1792, two Russian Czars (1762 and 1801), and unsuccessfully plotted the deposition of a third in 1825. Meanwhile, states without kings, like the Dutch Republic or the city republics of northern Italy, saw themselves as the very embodiment of freedom. But, as a noble visitor to Lucca observed in 1786,

> On one side the privilege of oppressing; on the other the necessity of suffering oppression: that is what they call here, as in all aristocracies or hundred-headed tyrannies, liberty. The word *libertas* is written in letters of gold over the town gates and on the corner of every street; and from reading the word so often, the people have come to believe they possess it.

The rhetoric of liberty was certainly inseparable from nobility. The very privileges that marked nobles off from others represented freedom from common burdens. This was not modern liberty, which means the absence of privilege, and rights equally shared by all. But it is hard to see how the latter could have taken shape without the older aristocratic tradition and the language in which it was couched. When the newer meaning began to emerge, in the course of the 17th and 18th centuries, it took the form of demands to extend to the many what only the few had hitherto enjoyed. The British, who had executed one king and expelled another for threatening their liberties, began to realize a century later that the main beneficiary had been an aristocratic oligarchy. The Americans, in renouncing their allegiance to the British crown in the name of liberty, took care in establishing their new republic to prohibit the establishment of any form of nobility; and within a decade the revolutionaries of France had made liberty and aristocracy seem like polar opposites.

The French Revolution began as a struggle to break the aristocratic grip on a national representative institution, the Estates-General. Yet parliamentary and representative institutions had themselves largely been the creation of medieval aristocracies. The English parliament originated in the continuing struggle of the barons who had humiliated King John to rein in the claims of his son. Nobles all over the Continent came to realize that representative bodies (particularly if they represented people like themselves) were more likely to be effective in restraining kings than sporadic rebellion, and rulers for their part recognized that to secure consent for their demands was better than facing down rebellions. Between the 12th and the 15th centuries, 'estates' or parliaments emerged in most of the polities of Western and Central Europe. They varied widely in composition, but most of them comprised a separate chamber or 'estate' for nobles, alongside the church, towns, or the 'Third Estate', and sometimes, as in Sweden, peasants. Almost inevitably nobles dominated them. In the Polish *sejm*, there were no non-nobles in either house. Houses of clergy usually included many noble bishops and abbots. Even in England, where the Commons (meaning *communes* not commoners) achieved precocious prominence, each county was represented by two 'knights', and membership and voting were extensively determined until the mid-19th century by the influence of peers in the House of Lords.

Called into being to strengthen government with the semblance of consent, above all to innovative taxation, parliaments and estates were soon enough attempting to withhold or mitigate consent, or make it conditional. They became bastions of 'aristocratic constitutionalism', airing grievances and resisting royal authority in the name of laws and privileges which mostly benefited only the ruling orders. Hard-pressed monarchs in the 16th century began to turn against them. They were convoked less and less often. Provincial estates frequently survived, but by the early 18th century the only kingdom-wide representative bodies meeting regularly and retaining real power – even that fluctuating markedly over time – were in Great Britain, Poland, Sweden, and Württemberg. Nobles ran them all, largely in their own interests, although they clothed their power in precedents and procedures which, particularly in the British case, were to provide models and templates for many later legislatures around the world. Even in France, where no Estates-General met between 1614 and 1789, a tradition of constitutional checks on monarchical power was kept alive by the *parlements*, courts of appeal with the right to protest against new laws. The magistrates in these courts were exclusively noble, and represented nothing except the power of the money which had bought their venal offices. But in France, as elsewhere, royal authority had weaned nobles from their attachment to representation by guaranteeing their other privileges. By 1789, they were eager to be represented again when a weakened monarch revived the Estates-General. But when they appeared determined at the same time to retain their other privileges, they opened themselves to attacks which would lead within months to the destruction of the noble order along with older organization of the Estates. All attempts to endow the National Assembly which now assumed sovereignty with features recalling the former Estates, or parliaments elsewhere, were voted down. Written constitutions, such as those now adopted here or in America, were designed as antidotes to aristocracy. And when, in Great Britain, the early 20th-century House of Lords proclaimed itself the 'watchdog of the constitution' while narrowly defending the landed interest, David Lloyd George could scoff that it was merely the ruling prime minister's poodle. Nine years later, now a minister himself, he would gleefully help to deprive the Lords of the last shreds of real political authority.

Religion

Aristocrats have usually been a mainstay of established churches. They have recognized that, although all are equal in the sight of God, St Paul enjoined Christians to obey those set over them. Organized religion endorsed and legitimized hierarchy and subordination, promising rewards hereafter for injustices and pains patiently endured in life. Or, as Napoleon put it with characteristic bluntness, the mystery of religion was the mystery of the social order. Religion imbued every aspect of medieval nobility and knighthood. Warriors commended their exertions to God; and crusading, to recapture the Holy Land from infidels or later simply to repel them from the frontiers of Christendom, was the highest cause to which true knights could commit themselves. And that vast majority who never went crusading could demonstrate their piety by endowing monasteries or chantries, granting or bequeathing land to be held for ever under the dead hand of the church, punctiliously and ostentatiously observing the sacraments. Increasingly too, they filled churches with their family monuments, and the more lucrative benefices with their family members or dependants. The huge wealth which the medieval church had accumulated by the early 16th century was mostly the result of its close involvement at every level with aristocratic power.

Nor did the sundering of the church at the Reformation weaken the relationship. Nobles were the main ultimate beneficiaries of the massive plunder of ecclesiastical wealth and dissolution of monasteries which occurred in realms which turned Protestant. It was as if they were repossessing wealth alienated to a church they no longer acknowledged. Once they had done so, they had a strong material interest in perpetuating the new order in religion. In the end, only small minorities of nobles held out against whatever creed became established in the realms where they lived, and the conforming majorities proved no friends to toleration, even of dissenting noble brethren. They seized control of even more ecclesiastical patronage, and when rising agricultural prices boosted the yield of the tithes which sustained the parish clergy to levels which lifted them out of penury, they infiltrated brothers and clients into the fattest livings. They liked bishops, sources like themselves of indisputable authority: in Great Britain, prelates sat alongside peers in the House of Lords. And when eventually they were forced to concede toleration to sects outside the establishment, they kept such democratic creeds at arm's length. Not for nothing did it come to be said that the Church of England was the Tory Party at prayer.

In countries that stayed Catholic, meanwhile, the aristocratic grip on the church remained as firm as ever. The ecclesiastical principalities of Germany, such as Cologne, Mainz, Trier, or Salzburg, were governed by bishops elected by chapters whose genealogical requirements for membership were among the most rigorous in Europe. Everywhere noble cadets colonized the best-endowed chapters and monasteries, while abbots and prioresses were the nominees of court patronage. All this meant that Catholic gentlemen could cheerfully disdain the hard work of cure of souls as parish priests. Lavish sums were spent on conventual buildings, reflecting their inmates' aristocratic taste. And aristocratic education remained overwhelmingly in clerical hands. Between the 1540s and the 1770s, the Jesuits almost monopolized the education of the elites of the Catholic world. In retrospect, their dissolution in 1773 came to seem like the first step towards the onslaught on all accepted values which marked the most extreme phase of the French Revolution. Certainly, to the revolutionaries of 1789, the 'privileged orders' of clergy and nobility were equal objects of attack. They were overthrown simultaneously, emerging from the revolutionary turmoil more than ever convinced of their common interests. Nineteenth-century Catholic aristocrats preferred to be privately educated by the clergy rather than by what they saw as godless state schools.

Even more than Protestant aristocracies, Catholic ones viewed toleration of rival creeds as a threat to their own hegemony. The first partition of Poland by foreign powers in 1772 was precipitated by a *Szlachta* confederation attempting to prevent concessions to Orthodox Christians along the Russian border. And the response of the Habsburgs to the defiance of the Protestant Bohemian nobility which began the Thirty Years War in the previous century was to supplant them with a new Catholic ruling class. The only

Protestant parallel was the systematic expropriation by the English of the Catholic gentry of Ireland over the 17th and 18th centuries for the benefit of a 'Protestant Ascendancy' closely modelled on the Anglican establishment across the water. But it made no serious attempt to evangelize the now-leaderless Catholics, and when support from London was gradually withdrawn over the 19th century, the Ascendancy found itself fatally isolated amid a hostile population.

Style and taste

Aristocratic ways and habits 'gave the tone' to the rest of society, and until the 19th century they set the dominant cultural norms and standards of the European world. As in the epics of antiquity, the heroes of medieval romance were invariably of good family, rich in valorous ancestors. Despite the scorn poured on knight-errantry by Cervantes's *Don Quixote* in the early 17th century, nobles were still devouring chivalric tales in the 18th, and with positively renewed enthusiasm in the 19th. At the theatre, and in that supreme entertainment designed to delight courtiers, opera, the leading characters were almost all noble. Not all could be heroes; but it was only towards the end of the 18th century that nobles began to be depicted as villains thwarted by the guile and courage of commoners. Until that time, too, the main patrons of serious music were nobles, whether as courtiers, amateur practitioners, or highly placed churchmen. Haydn, the ultimate musical retainer, was staggered to find on first visiting London in 1790 that the audience there for his music far transcended the nobility and gentry. Back in Vienna, the attempts of Mozart to survive in the open market without aristocratic patronage were only intermittently successful.

Aristocratic tastes similarly dominated the visual arts. If religious painting was conventionally ranked highest in importance, the best specimens were usually commissioned by rich and prestigious chapters or monasteries colonized by nobles, while secular patrons (at least before the Reformation humbled mortal pride) often demanded that they appear themselves in the scenes depicted. Next down came 'history painting', mostly devoted to episodes involving noble heroes of antiquity or legend with whom aristocrats instinctively identified. And then there were portraits, an essential element of noble interiors from the ancestral masks of the ancient Roman nobility down to the 'swagger portraits' of serried ancestors adorning halls and galleries from palaces to humble rural manor houses. No quality as important as ancestry could go visually unrecorded, and artists found that portraiture was incomparably the best paid and most reliable form of painting. For a non-noble to commission a portrait was a sure sign of social ambition. Another was to adorn surroundings with classical relics and décor, reflecting appreciation of the languages and history imbibed in the institutions of elite education. Grand tourists returned from Italy with implausible numbers of busts, torsos, and inscribed fragments, along with canvases, like gigantic picture postcards, depicting Rome, Naples, Venice, and other destinations of cultural pilgrimage.

Aristocrats were also the arbiters of more ephemeral fashion, in decoration, in furniture, in clothing, in pastimes, and even sometimes in speech. Until the 18th century, what Chesterfield called 'people of the first fashion' were undoubtedly courtiers. What the court did today, the world – or at least the world with disposable surpluses to spend – did tomorrow. The most striking example is perhaps that of wig-wearing. First introduced at the court of Louis XIV, and thereafter rapidly spreading to the rest of Europe, it lasted, with styles slowly evolving, until courts themselves shrank in size and importance in the age of the French Revolution. But by then, the rhythm of fashionable innovation was accelerating. The increasing commercialization which marked the 18th century was beginning to lead aristocratic fashion-setters as much as they themselves led, and courtly fashions were coming to seem dowdy and unappealing compared with the endless novelties now being peddled beyond that narrow world. The presumed well-filled pockets of lords and ladies were still the targeted market for purveyors of luxuries, but increasingly the suppliers formed the tastes of the consumers. By the early years of the next century, sartorial display for men at least had shrunk to the sphere of military uniforms. Only cut and quality of cloth now distinguished noble wearers of sober frock-coats from any other person of modest consequence. The days of aristocratic cultural hegemony were almost over.

And yet the memory lingered. The legacy was, after all, everywhere – in music, in art, in monuments, and, above all, perhaps, in buildings. The great houses of the higher nobility, in town or country, bear witness to the wealth, power, and prestige which their builders and inheritors once had. Country house building continued far into the 19th century, and all the advantages of new technology often made them larger and more lavish than ever. But classical models tended to be abandoned in favour of Gothic fantasies, harking back to times when aristocracy had been more unchallengeable than it had become since 1789. A century on from then, aristocrats were turning away from mansion building as their landed fortunes crumbled. Half a century later still, after the comparable upheaval of the First World War, they were abandoning them wholesale, demolishing them or selling them to institutions which alone could now cope with their size. Only after the Second World War did surviving seats still in private hands or made over to public or semi-public preservation organizations such as the National Trust or government heritage departments find a new destiny as museums of a vanished elite way of life.

Chapter 5
Aristocracy eclipsed

The myth among aristocrats that they stand for timeless values inherited from their ancestors has often dazzled and misled historians and other analysts who rely on them. They have tended to assume that when times or circumstances changed, hidebound aristocracies faced crises which challenged their very existence. It took many years for the realization to dawn that none of these supposed crises proved remotely fatal before the 20th century. But now the consensus is to emphasize how flexible and adaptable aristocracies have been when confronted with economic, institutional, or cultural change. The ways in which they managed this have been extensively studied. The final question is, therefore, not so much why a group making such irrational claims to power and authority could sustain them through endless vicissitudes, as why eventually it did succumb to a combination of forces which have left aristocracy as little more than a fragmented memory.

A master narrative for this process was offered by Marxism. Presupposing that the key to history is class struggle, and that classes are defined by their relationship to the means of production, Marxists see aristocrats as the feudal class. They dominated an agricultural economy and structure of society by extracting surplus from the helpless peasantry. But with the growth of towns, trade, and manufacturing, there emerged a middle class, or bourgeoisie, basing its wealth on capital and the exploitation of wage labour. Eventually, bourgeois economic power overtook that of the feudal class, and the great historical drama of early modern times was the transition from feudalism to capitalism, during which the bourgeoisie seized political power commensurate with its economic strength. The culminating moments were revolutions – whether the English in the 17th century or the French in the 18th – when aristocracy was violently overthrown.

Elegant and alluring though this analysis can be, and persuasively though it was fleshed out by the researches and arguments of left-wing scholars for much of the 20th century, it has failed to convince most historians. They have found the depiction of the English Civil War as a bourgeois revolution implausible, and using the same description for the French Revolution simplistic. They are struck by the extent to which aristocrats were involved in certain sorts of capitalism, and by the way rich bourgeois used their capital not to overthrow aristocracy, but to join it. Finally, they have noted that aristocracy survived even the French Revolution's attempt to destroy it, and that it was another century before aristocratic power began to ebb permanently away. The end of aristocracy was slower, messier, and more unpredictable than any grand theory of history allows for. And it was certainly much more of an eclipse than an overthrow.

Contestation

The rule of aristocrats, however firmly entrenched, has never gone uncontested. The early history of republican Rome was marked by determined and ultimately successful attempts by the plebeians to break the patrician monopoly of power. Then in 73 BC, the gladiator Spartacus led a slave uprising which briefly threatened the entire social structure of Roman Italy until his servile army was defeated by overwhelming military force. This has been the fate of most popular rebellions throughout history, but before their final defeat rebels have often taken brutal social revenge on their lords. The savagery of the French peasant revolt of 1358 gave a feared name to any subsequent uprising: *Jacquerie*. The English peasants' revolt of 1381 was far less bloody, but the rebels marched to the ominous slogan:

> When Adam delved, and Eve span
> Who was then the gentleman?

It terrified the memory of the upper classes for centuries. In Germany, the 'Peasants' War' which swept through many principalities in 1524–6 had the same effect, and with more justification. Many of the rebels' most pressing grievances were against the exactions of lords, and there was much destruction of noble property. But even this paled in comparison with the last phase of the great Pugachev uprising in Russia in 1774. Inspired by the defiant example of Cossacks resisting central authority, serfs along much of the length of the Volga struck out at nobles who had been steadily increasing their powers and exactions over preceding decades. Urged by Pugachev to massacre their lords and seize their property, peasant rebels hanged noblemen by the thousand and ravaged their property. Many more fled in terror. As one insurgent told a young noble captive: 'Your time is past'. It would be another century and a half before it was, as once again regular troops restored order. The reprisals which followed were even more savage – this too a standard pattern as returning lords purged their own terror. It was repeated when Transylvanian peasants massacred 3,000 nobles ten years later. The pattern was only broken in France at the end of that decade. Very few nobles were killed, although many were terrified, in the rural revolts which swept the French provinces in the spring and summer of 1789. But the instruments and symbols of noble power in the form of muniments, dovecotes, and even armorial weathervanes, were systematically targeted, and this time there was no army, and indeed no government to direct one, to put the outbreaks down. Instead, the newly formed National Assembly chose to appease the insurgents by decreeing the abolition of what they called feudalism – the whole structure of lordly rights and dues inherited from the Middle Ages. Thus began a chain of events which, less than a year later, would culminate in the Assembly decreeing the abolition of nobility itself. Yet the rebellious French peasants of 1789 had not called for this. Nor had most of the participants in preceding outbreaks elsewhere. Even rebels who slaughtered nobles scarcely glimpsed the possibility of a world without lords. What enraged them was not lordship as such, but abuse of it; nobles who did not behave as they should, who charged exorbitant rents, who changed the nature of their exactions, who made new and uncustomary demands, who entrusted their authority to profiteering middlemen, who neglected a duty of care to their tenants, vassals, or serfs.

The same was true of most intellectual opposition to the rule of nobles before the 18th century. Nobles were usually criticized not because their existence was wrong, but because they failed in various ways to live up to the high ideals which they professed and which were invoked to justify their position. Machiavelli, it is true, called them 'vermin'; but he was so reviled for other reasons that his strictures made little impact. More damage was perhaps done by the ridicule heaped by Cervantes on Don Quixote, whose head was addled by dreams of outmoded chivalry – yet his book was a great favourite with noble readers. It was the triumph in the 18th century of John Locke's contention that all men are born equal, biologically and mentally and not merely in the sight of God, that laid serious foundations for rejecting any claims to hereditary superiority. Only then did some of the classics which educated men read at school begin to echo more relevantly. Only then, for instance, could the sentiments of Marius, the first non-noble to achieve the consulship, in 111 BC, seem more relevant to modern times. As reported by Sallust, Marius had declared to the Roman people:

I believe that all men are partakers in one and the same nature, and that manly virtue is the only true nobility...Your ancestors won renown for themselves and for the state. Relying on that renown to shed a reflected glory on them,...noblemen, who are so different in character from these ancestors, despise us who emulate their virtues, and expect to receive all posts of honour at your hands, not because they deserve them, but as if they had a peculiar right to them. These proud men make a very big mistake. Their ancestors left them all they could – riches, portrait masks, and their own glorious memory. Virtue, they have not bequeathed to them, nor could they; for it is the only thing that no man can ever give to another or receive from another.

Even so, no coherent modern critique emerged before the American Revolution. Then, however, the new United States formally prohibited any titles of nobility as incompatible with republican institutions; and when officers in the Continental Army set up the hereditary Society of the Cincinnati to commemorate their achievement down the generations, it was fiercely denounced as the germ of an American aristocracy. Benjamin Franklin, American minister in Paris, had always declared that claims to hereditary distinction were 'a mere joke'. He produced calculations to show that little of any ancestor's blood flowed in anybody's veins after only a few generations. When news reached him of the controversy over the Cincinnati, he resolved to transmit the anti-aristocratic message to Europe. He persuaded the Count de Mirabeau, a renegade nobleman living by his pen, to produce a pamphlet ostensibly on the Cincinnati, but in reality an attack on nobility in general. *Considerations on the Order of Cincinnatus* appeared in 1784. Denouncing nobility as nothing more than a figment of opinion, Mirabeau condemned its bloody and tyrannical historical record, the pride and vanity which guided all so-called noble action, the folly of believing that distinction could be inherited, and the bad example of idleness and frivolity given to society at large. Nobility was an affront to natural equality, its members descended from brigands and now merely 'the titled

9. **Enemies of aristocracy: a) above; Honoré de Mirabeau (1749–91) and b) right; David Lloyd George (1863–1945). Lloyd George died an Earl, though he never took his seat in the House of Lords**

slaves of despots'. Here, five years before the French Revolution,
one destined to be among its early leaders denounced his own
order in comprehensive terms that fellow revolutionaries would
soon adopt as central to their entire ideology. America had shown
that a society without nobles was possible and workable. The
French were about to discover whether the same could be achieved
in Europe.

Revolution

The attack was not premeditated, nor did nobles expect it. Notoriously, it was nobles who did most to precipitate the crisis by their resistance, in a classic bout of aristocratic constitutionalism, to royal plans to avert bankruptcy. The only legitimate reforms, they contended, required the consent of the traditional representative body of the monarchy, the Estates-General. It had not met since 1614, but the forms observed then seemed to promise nobles the dominant collective role in government found across the Channel. They were represented in only one of the three chambers, but they were confident of managing the clergy through their control of the episcopate: and any two estates could outvote the third. But the prospect of the 'forms of 1614' provoked outrage among the literate Third Estate, who saw them as condemning 95% of the nation to perpetual legislative subjection to the so-called 'privileged orders'. The most famous pamphlet of the election campaign of 1789, Sieyès's *What is the Third Estate?*, argued that no privileged order could be part of the nation, and that the self-styled descendants of the Franks should go back to the German forests from whence they came. In response to the clamour, the king doubled the number of Third Estate deputies, but that meant nothing without vote by head. A minority of nobles sympathized with the Third, but most of those elected to the noble estate resisted any attempt to unite the orders into a single National Assembly until the Third unilaterally established one after six weeks of stalemate. Even then, it took a direct royal command to make the noble majority accept the end of separate orders. The result of eight months of controversy and noble resistance to the claims of the Third Estate was to unleash a bitter onslaught of suspicion and social antagonism. The words 'aristocrat' and 'aristocracy' became general terms denoting any sort of enemy of the Revolution. And in their original manifesto, the *Declaration of the Rights of Man and the Citizen* (26 August 1789), the revolutionaries proclaimed equality before the law, equality before the taxman, and equality of opportunity. 'Men are born', it declared, 'free and equal in rights. Social distinctions may be based only on common utility.' The privileged world of aristocratic domination was at an end.

The comprehensiveness of the challenge threw the French nobility into disarray. A minority welcomed the end of separate orders and attempted to cooperate in the complete recasting of national institutions. Many preferred to ride out the storm in passivity, hoping it would eventually subside. Another minority chose to emigrate, turning their backs on a country they no longer recognized as their own, and voicing increasingly bellicose threats from beyond the frontiers. The nobility as a whole was therefore in no state to resist the logical culmination of so much anti-aristocratic feeling and action when, on 20 June 1790, the National Assembly decreed the abolition of nobility itself, along with the use or display of titles, liveries, and coats of arms.

Liberal nobles took the lead on this occasion, deepening the rift with their fellows still further. But the tribulations of what now became known as *ci-devants* ('yesterday's people') were far from over. In 1791, even the king tried unsuccessfully to emigrate. His example encouraged many who had so far resisted what those already gone called 'the road of honour'. It was the antics of the *émigrés*, calling themselves alone the nobility, which pushed the revolutionaries into war against the German powers in 1792. Protected by the enemy, they now became traitors, their lands were confiscated, and eventually so were those of their relatives who had remained behind. When the war went badly, all remaining former nobles fell under suspicion; and in the Terror of 1793–4, 1,200 lost their heads. It was less than 1% of their number, and the guillotine claimed the lives of far more ordinary people. But the public humiliation and execution of so many members of the former ruling order was a spectacular demonstration of aristocratic vulnerability. Never before in history had the power

10. Anti-aristocratic propaganda in the French Revolution: a) above; a peasant carries the burden of the privileged on his back, while others (b) right; celebrate the abolition of feudalism by pulverizing the symbols of nobility

and glory of nobility been so completely challenged, demonized, and overthrown. Nobody had ever imagined it could be done. Now that the unthinkable had happened, the possibility was always there to tempt the ambition of radicals, reformers, and other revolutionaries, and to haunt surviving aristocrats everywhere. The myth that there was no alternative to the rule of hereditary landed elites was shattered for ever.

Rank closes ranks

Yet abolition failed. When the Terror ended, noble *émigrés* began to drift cautiously back, and find ways of recovering their lost properties. When Napoleon (a nobleman who had been made rather than destroyed by the Revolution) took power, he swiftly

11. Charles-Maurice de Talleyrand (1754–1838), a pre-revolutionary
nobleman transformed into a Napoleonic prince

invited anyone not committed to the deposed Bourbon dynasty to return and serve him. When he made himself an emperor, he wanted to surround himself with courtiers, and he created a new titled elite. He claimed it was not a nobility, and said it was intended to supplant the remnants of the old one; but he was keen to recruit *ci-devants* into it, and when he fell, the restored Bourbons recognized this six-year-old creation as the real thing.

Nobles of pre-revolutionary lineage sneered. They alone, they thought, were authentic. And privately they had never recognized the National Assembly's right or even power to abolish a status which they had inherited in the blood of their ancestors and that not even God could take away from them. What the revolutionaries had been able to abolish was public recognition for nobility and its main avenues of recruitment. They had, therefore, turned the most open nobility in Europe into a closed caste. Access reopened during the 15 years of the restoration, but pre-revolutionary rhythms of recruitment were never restored. After 1830, ennoblements slowed to a trickle, and with the final triumph of republicanism after 1870, they dried up entirely.

Meanwhile, the appalling spectacle of France's anti-aristocratic revolution struck fear into every other European nobility. Suddenly they all felt threatened. So did monarchs. The plans of Emperor Joseph II to undermine the power of lords in his hereditary lands by emancipating the serfs, formulated in the 1760s and pursued throughout the 1780s, were rapidly abandoned even before he died in 1790. Catherine the Great of Russia declared that her job was to be an aristocrat. In Prussia, a new law code of 1794 consolidated nobles' prerogatives and their power over their serfs, while Swedish nobles assassinated a king who appeared determined to foster democratic aspirations. In England, Edmund Burke, for most of his life dependent on the patronage of peers, denounced the French Revolution in comprehensive terms, and its attack on 'the Corinthian capital of polished society' as the work of a 'sour, malignant envious disposition, without taste for the reality or for any image or representation of virtue'. And if he was opposed and outsold by Tom Paine's *Rights of Man*, with its lampooning of nobility as 'no-ability', Burke's *Reflections on the Revolution in France* was translated into most major European languages and became the international bible of social and institutional conservatism.

Buoyed by their initial victories over the noble-led armies of Prussia and Austria, in 1792 the French revolutionaries proclaimed their war aims as *War on the Castles, Peace to the Cottages*! They committed themselves to overturning the social system of the countries they overran. Proportionately, however, the cottages suffered more than the castles. No level of society went unscathed when French invaders arrived, and as a result of the French wars certain noble-ruled states, such as the city republics of Italy or the prince bishoprics of Germany, disappeared for ever. So did the Holy Roman Empire, much of whose business over its last century had concerned the rights and prerogatives of the various forms of nobility existing under its umbrella. Many former sovereign princelings found their territories 'mediatized' into components of larger kingdoms, and themselves left with mere hollow titles and dignities. And the morale of the militaristic Prussian *Junkers* was temporarily shattered by their defeat by Napoleon in 1806. But when conquest was succeeded by occupation or other forms of control, the French found there was no real substitute to working through existing elites and their networks of authority. Initial attempts by Prussian reformers to free serfs and open careers to the talents in order to combat the French with the same energies that the Revolution had released, were blunted by widespread *Junker* opposition. So that when Napoleon was eventually defeated by an international coalition, the mass armies involved were still largely officered by noblemen, and his downfall was widely regarded as a triumph for the forces of social conservatism. Aristocrats in all countries were determined to use their victory to ensure that the challenge just overcome should never be repeated.

Indian summer

But the pre-revolutionary world could not be rebuilt. A spell had been broken. The rule of aristocrats had been shown to be vulnerable, and any attempt to make it less so inevitably changed its very character. A coherent anti-noble ideology now existed, and was known to be feasible. The age-old claims of nobility could all be rationally refuted. There was also now a confident and receptive audience for anti-noble arguments, and it was expanding. Ideas of natural and civil equality could only be of benefit to an educated middle class growing at unprecedented speed with economic expansion and burgeoning state power. Commoners enriched by trade or manufacture, or dignified by office-holding, remained susceptible to the allure of buying land and adopting noble lifestyles, but increasing numbers were inspired by the example of the French Third Estate in 1789, taking power to create the most powerful state in Europe in the teeth of noble selfishness and disdain. Not only, therefore, did they reject aristocratic claims to hereditary social distinction. They also opposed the age-old noble monopoly of political authority, demanding representative institutions or, if they already had them, wider representation for men of property, wealth, and talent but possessing no hereditary credentials. This was not yet a call for complete democracy, although it was often called that. But it was certainly a rejection of any sort of aristocracy.

Nobles never underestimated the challenge, but as in France in 1789, they could not agree on how to meet it. The instinct of most was to dig in, make no concessions, and seek ways of protecting themselves against what they saw as the weaknesses that had brought about their tribulations. Others saw this stance as suicidal. Faced with a rapidly changing world, they must 'reform that they might preserve', or, as the fictional Sicilian prince puts it in 1860 in Lampedusa's novel *The Leopard*: 'If we want things to stay as they are, things will have to change.' The great parliamentary Reform

Bill of 1832, resisted to the last by the British House of Lords, destroyed the political influence of many peers and gave representation for the first time to burgeoning industrial cities, but it was defended by the prime minister Earl Grey as harmless to 'the real interests of the aristocracy'. Similar arguments were advanced in defence of serf emancipation, which occurred throughout Eastern Europe and Germany between 1807 and 1864. While diehards raged against the idea of former subjects becoming free proprietors alongside them, now able to own lands formerly designated as noble, and predicted economic doom without the benefit of free labour services, reformers argued that the end of lordship would make it easier for greater landowners to profit from the expanding market for agricultural goods in a century of soaring population. The end of an unjust system of subjection, they also implied, would make the lower classes in the countryside less likely to challenge the established order. Serf uprisings in Hungary in 1831, or Galicia in 1846, underlined the lesson, and the paralysis of central authorities during the revolutions of 1848 brought renewed rural anarchy. To calm it, the Austrian Emperor decreed emancipation in all his domains, and was rapidly followed in most smaller German principalities. Despite the complexities and disappointments for all sides which implementation of emancipation entailed, peasant unrest was dramatically defused.

Although the fleeting second French Republic briefly renewed the 1790 abolition of nobility, the revolutions of 1848 were primarily directed against monarchs rather than aristocracies. When the upheavals were over, kings and nobles reforged their old alliance, grudgingly joining hands with propertied non-nobles who had been equally scared by the socialistic rhetoric which had been unleashed. In the various liberal constitutions adopted over subsequent decades, there was normally provision, based on the admired stability of the British model, for a lower house elected from property owners, and a nominated or hereditary upper chamber of aristocrats. In these ways, nobles continued to play a prominent, sometimes still dominant though no longer monopolistic, role in the public life of all European states. Only by shunning it altogether, like the French Legitimists who after the downfall of the senior Bourbon line in 1830 preferred 'internal emigration', could they now avoid dealings with the ever more assertive middle classes. But the bond of property increasingly drew them together, and the agricultural prosperity of the mid-19th century meant that landowners of any size did well. Former lords were often able to swallow up the unviable plots which their serfs received on emancipation. In Spain, the abolition in the 1830s of the *mayorazgo* did not lead as expected and intended to the break-up of the notorious Iberian *latifundia*, any more than the repeal of the British corn laws in 1846 brought the predicted ruin of the 'landed interest'. Nobles were also now investing as never before in new or expanding industries, such as railways or coal. With the creaking exception of Russia, aristocrats by the mid-19th century had lost most of the residual trappings of feudalism – organization into a legal order, jurisdiction over vassals (serf or otherwise), exemption and privileges of all sorts. Now they signalled their superiority by paying more tax, not less. But their social ascendancy was still widely acknowledged and deferred to, their titles or status still legally recognized, and their involvement in the exercise of power and authority pervasive. After the most serious crisis in its history, aristocracy appeared once more to have survived, wounded but still walking.

The agony of aristocracy

Just as the first open onslaught on aristocracy was signalled by European echoes of the Cincinnati controversy in America, transatlantic conflicts also heralded its final retreat. At the very moment when the serfs of Russia, the last major servile population in Europe, were being granted their freedom in 1861, the United States was locked in a civil war over ending slavery. Slavery had enabled the planters of the old South to live in ways which mimicked the lifestyles of aristocratic Europe. The defeat of the Confederacy brought the end of this world. It also unlocked the agricultural and industrial strength of the re-United States. By 1869, within four years of the Union victory, the Atlantic and Pacific had been linked by railways. Steam and steel released the vast agricultural potential of the prairies, and then that of other extra-European territories, whether by railways or ever-larger steamships, eventually with refrigeration. These technologies flooded Europe with cheap food, plunging agriculture into a generation of depression. There was a brief revival in the first decade of the 20th century, but no sustained recovery until after the Second World War.

The pressure from agricultural lobbies to impose protective tariffs shows how strong landed elites still were. Most governments caved in to them, although the national markets eventually protected scarcely compensated for lost export outlets. The major exception was Great Britain, where free trade was now an orthodoxy, and voters had grown used to cheap food. Here landed revenues were allowed to plummet. Attempts by Irish landowners to compensate by raising rents were met by a peasant 'land war' which governments only calmed by enacting changes which opened the way to the virtual expropriation of the landed Ascendancy. In England, meanwhile, country house building was largely abandoned, and owners began to sell land and other assets such as libraries or works of art, putting whatever profits they made in a depressed market into the sort of liquid assets that most of their ancestors would have shunned. And no sooner had conditions began to ease in the 1890s, than estate duty was introduced to tax capital assets as well as income. Within ten years, Lloyd George, who hated and despised the landed aristocracy, had begun as Chancellor of the Exchequer to impose yet heavier taxes on them, eventually provoking the House of Lords into its fatal resistance to his 1909 budget.

The cry of 'peers against the people' had been in the air ever since the Lords had tried to block the widening of the parliamentary franchise in the 1880s. They saw clearly enough that democracy

12. British blue blood marries American millions: the family of the ninth Duke of Marlborough, by John Singer Sargent

would be fatal to all they stood for. Three decades earlier, the Marquess of Salisbury, destined to be the last British prime minister to govern from the Lords, declared that 'The classes that represent civilisation . . . have a right to require securities to protect them from being overwhelmed by hordes who have neither knowledge to guide them nor stake in the commonwealth to control them.' Time would teach him that they had no such right. As the historian Alexis de Tocqueville (1805–59), aristocratic to his fingertips, but the most clear-eyed observer of his age, put it at the same moment, the world was now driven 'by an unknown force – which may possibly be regulated or moderated, but cannot be overcome – towards the destruction of aristocracies'.

Agrarian elites were being remorselessly undermined by the industrial world. As changes in transport technology pulverized traditional forms of wealth, men made rich by finance, trade, and industry were now, for the first time in history, richer than even the greatest landlords. Noble families whom chance had endowed with coal or mineral deposits, or estates in the path of expanding cities, might continue to amass fabulous fortunes, but the rest were increasingly outshone by men of business. And if the latter still acquired country houses, they did not maintain them by the profits of agriculture. Meanwhile, throughout much of Europe the educated middle class, in unprecedented numbers, was being admitted into the elites through ennoblement, and, even without that, penetrating the upper ranks of bureaucracies and the armed forces as never before. If the heights of command were still spectacularly and overwhelmingly in traditional hands, ranks that had previously been virtual noble monopolies now had majorities of non-nobles, if only because they were expanding at rates which noble numbers could not possibly match.

Then came the First World War. It has been argued that this conflict began as a determined attempt by Europe's aristocracies to reassert their faltering hegemony. It was an 'aristocratic reaction' whose 'inner spring . . . was the over-reaction of old elites to overperceived dangers to their over-privileged positions' and 'the old ruling and governing classes ... meant to resolve Europe's crisis in their own interest, if need be by induced war'. Most historians have found this thesis more stimulating than convincing. But even if rescuing aristocracy from the forces of the modern world had been what the war was supposed to achieve, the miscalculation was massive. It merely accelerated all the trends which had been sapping aristocratic power and authority for almost half a century. Trench warfare proved a holocaust of young officers, decimating a generation of heirs to famous names in all the countries involved. The war precipitated the Russian Revolution, a consciously anti-aristocratic movement which resulted in the wholesale confiscation and redistribution of noble estates and the persecution of their owners, scattering *émigrés* across Western Europe and beyond. In the war's aftermath, monarchies disappeared throughout Germany and Central Europe, and the precarious republics which succeeded them abolished noble titles and the entails which had kept aristocratic estates together. New nation-states emerging from the break-up of the Habsburg Empire saw the great magnate dynasties which had dominated them for so long as relics of alien rule, and dispossessed them accordingly. Only in Poland and Hungary did aristocracy emerge reinvigorated, as re-created sovereign states turned once more to the native elites who had preserved the tradition of their former 'golden freedoms'. But even here the resurrection proved fleeting. The bravery of the resurgent *Szlachta* proved unavailing against invading Germans and Russians in the Second World War, and in its aftermath both Poland and Hungary succumbed to Communist regimes which, as in Russia, were determined to wipe out every relic of aristocratic rule.

The break-up of the United Kingdom of Great Britain and Ireland was almost as traumatic. In Ireland, where the landed power of the Ascendancy had been eroding fast even before the war, the establishment of the Free State was accompanied by widespread attacks on country houses, and followed by the final expropriation of most of the landlords: an annihilation almost as complete as that in Russia. Across the water, as death duties on land were raised during and after the war to punitive levels, demoralized landowners offloaded more acres between 1918 and 1922 than had changed hands in a comparable period since the 1530s. Great houses were increasingly seen as costly white elephants, and large numbers were sold, demolished, or, from the late 1930s, offered to the National Trust in return for continued family tenancy. Though the richest, mostly ducal, families remained despite shrinking estates among the wealthiest in the country, the old gentry dwindled away and the aristocracy as a whole became spectacularly demoralized. A few who had sold out moved to the African colonies where they could still live relatively cheaply, hunt wild animals freely, and keep abundant retinues of docile servants; but even these alluring retreats from the modern world would scarcely last more than a few decades as the Empire, too, which had afforded younger sons so many opportunities for more than two centuries, crumbled.

Another reflex of embattled aristocrats between the wars was to toy with Fascism. After all, Communism and other forms of Socialism (they scarcely differentiated between them) had proved the most implacable enemies they had. The various forms of Fascism by contrast promised vigorously restored order. The Spanish aristocracy was indeed rescued from democratic threats by the victory of Franco in the Civil War, so that the restoration of monarchy itself seemed entirely logical after his death. In German-speaking lands, too, many noble army officers welcomed Hitler's restoration of military self-esteem. But his disastrous wartime policies eventually provoked a handful of shame-faced officers to try to assassinate him. It was (so far!) the last aristocratic conspiracy in European history. But by the time it failed, Hitler's defeat in any case already seemed all but inevitable. A decisive second front had been launched against German-occupied Europe from Great Britain, where Winston Churchill, grandson of a duke, and a clutch of mainly Irish patrician generals (all rewarded with

13. Nobles and Nazis: Adolf Hitler with Unity Mitford, daughter of Lord Redesdale

titles and seats in the House of Lords) had led a determined and sometimes desperate struggle for national survival. But the war was really won by powers which had renounced aristocracy and all its ways: the USA and the USSR. And Churchill's reward for saving his country was to be voted out of office by his democratic compatriots. Nine years later, before he left office for the last time, Queen Elizabeth II offered him a dukedom. It was an empty enough gesture, though flattering, since she had ascertained in advance that he would refuse. Ironically, Attlee, the commoner who had replaced him as prime minister in 1945, ended up as an earl.

Relics, memories, verdicts

Thus the Second World War completed the destruction of aristocracy as a coherent entity of social or political understanding. In the war's aftermath, Communist takeovers finally sealed its fate

14. The British Coronation, 1953: beleaguered peers run for cover

throughout Eastern Europe, and the democratic socialist regimes which periodically gained power in the West proved scarcely more sympathetic. The last institutional redoubt of aristocratic power, the British House of Lords, lost most of its residual legislative delaying power at the hands of a Labour government in 1948, most of its hereditary members at the hands of another half a century later, and seems set to lose the last of them as this book goes to press.

Plenty of aristocrats can still be found. The princes of Liechtenstein and Monaco, once vassals of great monarchs, now rule tiny sovereign states. The richest man and the greatest landowner in Great Britain are both dukes. Everywhere a title or even a coat of arms retains a certain cachet, and companies remain pleased to have a 'lord on the board'. Aristocrats still prefer to inter-marry, although they can no more resist a rich heiress from outside than they ever could. They still prefer to send their children to a handful of prestigious private schools. And although most now earn their livings in every conceivable walk of life, in leisure they still enjoy the highest profile in hunting, horse-racing, field sports, and country life in general. But with hereditary ennoblement now discontinued everywhere, the fate of these closed castes will be slowly to dwindle away to nothing.

Yet the physical and visual relics of their ancestors, personal or collective, can be found everywhere in monuments, inscriptions, tombs, street and pub names, parklands, and, above all, country houses or 'stately homes'. Despite the disappearance of hundreds of them during the 20th century, there are still enough left to remind the citizens of democracies whose establishment most of their owners bitterly resented, of who once gave orders to their own ancestors. Many are now open to a paying public, and their surviving owners have created a new vocation for themselves as custodians of a cultural heritage supposedly built up with exquisite care by generations of forebears. Many of those forebears were in fact little more than routine accumulators, and many more, often quite recently, have been indifferent to the quality of what they inherited and seen it as a positive burden. Nevertheless, the artistic and cultural wealth which these residences house and represent is still, despite over a century of economic and political ravages, impressive and sometimes awe-inspiring. It is evidence of how down the centuries aristocrats have been able to exploit and profit from the labours of others for their own comfort and advantage. Yet often, it is not the pictures, artefacts, and decorative displays which seem to make most impact on modern visitors. They are far more interested in the kitchens and other 'below stairs' domestic arrangements. These they can far more readily identify with, aware that the servants' hall was the place for their own ancestors, born to wait upon the pride and arrogance of those who lived above.

For, despite residual and sporadic instincts of deference, few modern people have any belief in innate superiorities. They dislike anything hinting that it is still being claimed. They have little time for 'feudal remnants', as a young daughter of the peppery Lord Redesdale once imprudently described him to his face. Actually, as a mere second-generation baron, like most aristocrats he was no such thing. But aristocrats love to cover their more distant tracks, which are often rooted in violence, greed, and ruthless exploitation of those weaker than themselves. The diarist James Lees-Milne, son of an industrialist masquerading as a landed gentleman, but educated (Eton, Oxford, and the Guards) to become a real one, devoted his long life to saving country houses. He met their owners almost on a daily basis, and knew some of the grandest intimately. His opinion therefore commands respect. 'I have come to the conclusion,' he wrote in 1996, the year before he died, 'that the aristocracy have always been shits, and that in my youth I was too beguiled by them. Nevertheless, I still maintain that the decent and educated ones attain a standard of well-being and good-doing which has never been transcended by any other class in the world.'

References

Chapter 1

Plato, *The Republic*, iv.

Aristotle, *Politics*, iii, 7; iv, 6; ii, 11; iv, 7; iv, 8.

Montesquieu, *De'Esprit des Lois* (1748), ii, 4.

Charles Loyseau, *A Treatise of Orders and Plain Dignities* (1610; ed. and tr. Howell A. Lloyd, 1994), 111.

Frederick A. Pottle (ed.), *Boswell on the Grand Tour: Germany and Switzerland, 1764* (1953), 116.

Chapter 2

M. L. Bush, *The English Aristocracy: A Comparative Synthesis* (1984), 4.

Quotation of 1790 in William Doyle, *Aristocracy and Its Enemies in the Age of Revolution* (2009), 241.

Marquis de Mirabeau, *L'Ami des Hommes* (1762 edn.), i, 123.

The Complete Letters of Lady Mary Wortley Montagu, ed. Robert Halsband, 3 vols (1965), i, 257.

Blaise de Monluc, cited in Lucien Bély (ed.), *Dictionnaire de l'Ancien Régime* (1996), 641.

Montesquieu, *Esprit des Lois*, iii, 6–8; iv, 2.

Chapter 3

Duc de Lévis, *Maximes et Réflexions* (1808), no. 73.

Ruskin, quoted in Richard Mullen and James Munson, *The Smell of the Continent: The British Discover Europe* (2009).

Baldassare Castiglione, *The Book of the Courtier* (Everyman edn., 1965), 68–9.

Cardinal Richelieu, *Maximes d'État ou Testament Politique* (1974), 198.

Earl of Chesterfied, *Letters Written by the Earl of Chesterfield to His Son, Philip Stanhope* (1774), 12 October 1748.

Napoleon, quoted in J. Christopher Herold, *The Mind of Napoleon* (1955), 14.

Duchess (now dowager) of Bedford (then Marchioness of Tavistock) in the television series *Country House* (2000).

Chapter 4

Constantia Maxwell (ed.), *Arthur Young, A Tour in Ireland* (1925), 190–1.

Alexander Herzen, *Childhood, Youth, and Exile* (1956), 73–4.

The consumption of great Parisian familes in Natacha Coquéry, *L'Hôtel aristocratique: Le marché de luxe à Paris au xviiie siècle* (1998).

Marquis d'Argens, *Lettres Juives* (1738), iv, 15–16.

Adam Smith, *An Enquiry into the Nature and Causes of the Wealth of Nations* (1776), ii, 3.

On public school education, Martin Wiener, *English Culture and the Decline of the Industrial Spirit, 1850–1980* (1981).

Montaigne, quoted in Stuart Carroll, *Noble Power during the French Wars of Religion: The Guise Affinity and the Catholic Cause in Normandy* (1998), 255.

C. J. B. M. Mercier-Dupaty, *Lettres sur l'Italie* (1788), letter xxiii.

Chesterfield, *Letters to His Son*, 12 November 1750.

Chapter 5

Paul Avrich, *Russian Rebels, 1600–1800* (1972), 237.

Niccolò Machiavelli, *The Discourses*, ed. Bernard Crick (1970), 245–6.

Sallust, *The Jugurthine War*, tr. S. A. Handford (1963), 118, 120.

Benjamin Franklin: Writings, ed. J. A. Leo Lemay (1987), 1269.

Considerations on the Order of Cincinnatus, translated from the French of the Count de Mirabeau (1785), 78.

Edmund Burke, *Reflections on the Revolution in France* (1790), 205.

Thomas Paine, *Rights of Man* (1791–2; 1915 edn.), 90.

Giuseppe di Lampedusa, *The Leopard* (English tr., 1960), 28.

Marquess of Salisbury, quoted in Dominic Lieven, *The Aristocracy in Europe, 1815–1914* (1992), 237.

Alexis de Tocqueville, quoted in David Cannadine, *The Decline and Fall of the British Aristocracy* (1990), 698–9.

Arno J. Mayer, *The Persistence of the Old Regime: Europe to the Great War* (1981), 304–5.

Jessica Mitford, *Hons and Rebels* (1977), 57.

James Lees-Milne, *The Milk of Paradise: Diaries, 1993–1997* (2005), 203, 3 January 1996.

Further reading

Most European history written before the 20th century is incidentally the history of aristocrats. History was about power and its exercise, and that had always been an aristocratic monopoly. Only when aristocratic power was in full retreat were the history or activities of other groups recognized as important; and then, curiously, the new social history seemed to involve the study of everything but traditional elites. Research on nobilities as such took off relatively late. But since the middle of the last century, an expanding flow of case studies has examined every aspect of noble behaviour in a wide range of chronological and geographical contexts, dispelling many of the self-serving myths upon which earlier impressions and assumptions about that behaviour were based. No brief book list can indicate more than a small and arbitrary selection from this work. Everything listed here is in English, even though important material has been published in several other languages. Those who can read those languages will normally find the most important items in the bibliographies and footnotes of more specialist studies.

General

T. B. Bottomore, *Elites and Society* (1964). Lucid introduction to the study of elites in general, putting aristocracies into context.

Michael Bush, *Noble Privilege* (1983) and *Rich Noble, Poor Noble* (1988). First two volumes of an unfinished trilogy, *The European Nobility*, a quite indispensable compendium of comparative information.

Jack Goody, Joan Thirsk, and E. P. Thompson (eds.), *Family and Inheritance: Rural Society in Western Europe, 1200–1800* (1976). Contains essays of first-rate importance.

Frederic Cople Jaher (ed.), *The Rich, the Well Born and the Powerful* (1973). Wide chronological range of informative essays.

Robert Lacey, *Aristocrats* (1983). Book of a popular television series on rich surviving families.

Michael Mann, *The Sources of Social Power* (2 vols, 1986–93). Worldwide comparisons.

Barrington Moore, Jr, *Social Origins of Dictatorship and Democracy: Lord and Peasant in the Making of the Modern World* (1966). More worldwide comparisons.

Jonathan Powis, *Aristocracy* (1984). Brief, elegant, and thoughtful pioneering synthesis.

Ancient

M. T. W. Arnheim, *Aristocracy in Greek Society* (1977).

P. A. Brunt, *The Fall of the Roman Republic* (1988). Modern treatment of episodes that have haunted all aristocratic history.

M. Gelzer, *The Roman Nobility* (English tr., 1969). Classic analysis.

R. E. Mitchell, *Patricians and Plebeians* (1991).

C. G. Starr, *The Aristocratic Temper of Greek Civilisation* (1992).

Ronald Syme, *The Roman Revolution* (1939). A classic, now somewhat superseded by Brunt (above).

Medieval

Perry Anderson, *Passages from Antiquity to Feudalism* (1974). Bravura Marxism.

Marc Bloch, *Feudal Society*, 2 vols (English tr., 1961). Classic survey, now superseded in many respects.

Georges Duby, *The Three Orders: Feudal Society Imagined* (English tr., 1980).

Maurice Keen, *Chivalry* (1984).

Timothy Reuter (ed.), *The Medieval Nobility* (1978). Wide-ranging translated essays.

M. G. A. Vale, *War and Chivalry: Warfare and Aristocratic Culture in England, France and Burgundy at the End of the Middle Ages* (1981).

Chris Wickham, *The Inheritance of Rome: A History of Europe 400–1000* (2009). Up-to-date survey, strong on the murky origins of noble power.

Heyday

Perry Anderson, *Lineages of the Absolutist State* (1974). Another dazzling Marxist synthesis.

Ronald G. Asch, *Nobilities in Transition, 1550–1700: Courtiers and Rebels in Britain and Europe* (1993).

Samuel Clark, *State and Status: The Rise of the State and Aristocratic Power in Western Europe* (1995).

Jonathan Dewald, *The European Nobility, 1400–1800* (1996).

A. Goodwin (ed.), *The European Nobility in the Eighteenth Century* (1953). Pioneering collection in its day. Not all the contributions yet superseded.

Jerzy Lukowski, *The European Nobility in the Eighteenth Century* (2003). Excellent and up-to-date survey.

H. M. Scott (ed.), *The European Nobilities in the Seventeenth and Eighteenth Centuries*, 2nd edn. (2007). Unrivalled compendium of authoritative essays, well balanced between Eastern and Western Europe.

Hillay Zmora, *Monarchy, Aristocracy and the State in Europe, 1300–1800* (2001).

Eclipse

Jerome Blum, *The End of the Old Order in Rural Europe* (1978). Wide-ranging, if conceptually debatable.

William Doyle, *Aristocracy and its Enemies in the Age of Revolution* (2009). Chronicles early attacks on nobilities.

Dominic Lieven, *The Aristocracy in Europe, 1815–1914* (1992). Invaluable comparative survey.

Arno J. Mayer, *The Persistence of the Old Regime: Europe to the Great War* (1981). Challenging and controversial.

D. Spring (ed.), *European Landed Elites in the Nineteenth Century* (1997).

Karina Urbach, *European Aristocracies and the Radical Right, 1918–1939* (2007).

Ellis Wasson, *Aristocracy and the Modern World* (2006). Extremely useful overview.

Country by country

Great Britain

J. V. Beckett, *The Aristocracy in England, 1660–1914* (1986). Judicious and well informed.

M. L. Bush, *The English Aristocracy: A Comparative Synthesis* (1984). Argues convincingly against English exceptionalism.

David Cannadine, *The Decline and Fall of the British Aristocracy* (1990). Huge and magnificent chronicle of aristocratic downfall.

John Cannon, *Aristocratic Century: The Peerage of Eighteenth Century England* (1984).

John Habbakuk, *Marriage, Debt and the Estates System: English Landownership 1650–1950* (1994). Definitive analysis of property management.

K. B. Macfarlane, *The Nobility of Later Medieval England* (1973). Demythologizes the Wars of the Roses.

G. E. Mingay, *The Gentry: The Rise and Fall of a Ruling Class* (1976).

Lawrence Stone, *The Crisis of the Aristocracy, 1558–1641* (1965; abridged edn., 1967). Monumental if controversial backdrop to the Civil War.

Lawrence Stone and Jeanne C. Fawtier Stone, *An Open Elite? England 1540–1880* (1984).

Ireland

Toby Barnard, *A New Anatomy of Ireland: The Irish Protestants, 1649–1770* (2003).

J. C. Beckett, *The Anglo-Irish Tradition* (1976).

A. P. W. Malcomson, *The Pursuit of the Heiress: Aristocratic Marriage in Ireland, 1740–1840*, 2nd edn. (2006).

France

William H. Beik, *Absolutism and Society in Seventeenth Century France: State Power and Provincial Aristocracy in Languedoc* (1985). Challenges traditional interpretations of Louis XIV's relations with nobles.

Guy Chaussinand-Nogaret, *The French Nobility in the Eighteenth Century: From Feudalism to Enlightenment* (English tr., 1985).

Another challenge to traditional interpretations. Remains controversial.

Jonathan Dewald, *Aristocratic Experience and the Origins of Modern Culture: France, 1570–1715* (1993).

William Doyle, *Venality: The Sale of Offices in Eighteenth Century France* (1996). Much material on ennoblement by office.

Robert Forster, *The House of Saulx-Tavanes: Versailles and Burgundy, 1700–1830* (1971).

Robert R. Harding, *Anatomy of a Power Elite: The Provincial Governors of Early Modern France* (1979).

David Higgs, *Nobles in Nineteenth Century France: The Practice of Inegalitarianism* (1987).

Mark Motley, *Becoming a French Aristocrat: The Education of the Court Nobility, 1580–1715* (1990).

Ellery Schalk, *From Valor to Pedigree: Ideas of Nobility in Sixteenth and Seventeenth Century France* (1986).

Jay M. Smith, *The Culture of Merit: Nobility, Royal Service, and the Culture of Absolute Monarchy, 1600–1789* (1996).

Jay M. Smith (ed.), *The French Nobility in the Eighteenth Century: Reassessments and New Approaches* (2006).

Germany

B. Arnold, *German Knighthood, 1050–1300* (1985).

Thomas M. Barker, *Army, Aristocracy and Monarchy: Essays on War, Society and Government in Austria, 1618–1780* (1982).

Robert M. Berdahl, *The Politics of the Prussian Nobility, 1770–1848* (1988).

Otto Brunner, *Land and Lordship: Structures of Governance in Medieval Austria* (English tr., 1992).

F. L. Carsten, *A History of the Prussian Junkers* (1989).

R. J. W. Evans, *The Making of the Habsburg Monarchy, 1550–1700* (1979).

William D. Godsey, Jr, *Nobles and Nation in Central Europe: Free Imperial Knights in the Age of Revolution, 1750–1850* (2004).

Gregory Pedlow, *The Survival of the Hessian Nobility, 1770–1870* (1989). Offers a wider view than the title promises.

Hans Rosenberg, *Bureaucracy, Aristocracy and Autocracy: The Prussian Experience 1660–1815* (1958).

R. Gates-Coon, *The Landed Estates of the Esterházy Princes* (1994).

Italy

Tommaso Astarita, *The Continuity of Feudal Power: The Carraciolo di Brienza in Spanish Naples* (1992).

R. Burr Litchfield, *Emergence of a Bureaucracy: The Florentine Patricians, 1530–1790* (1986).

J. C. Davis, *The Decline of the Venetian Nobility as a Ruling Class* (1962).

Gregory Hanlon, *The Twilight of a Military Tradition: Italian Aristocrats and European Conflicts, 1560–1800* (1997).

Holland

H. K. F. Van Nierop, *The Nobility of Holland: From Knights to Regents, 1500–1650* (1993).

Sweden

Michael Roberts, *Essays in Swedish History* (1967). Contains an important essay on Aristocratic Constitutionalism.

Michael Roberts, *The Age of Liberty: Sweden 1719–1772* (1986).

Poland and Eastern Europe

J. K. Fedorowicz (ed.), *A Republic of Nobles: Studies in Polish History to 1864* (1982).

Jerzy Lukowski, *Liberty's Folly: The Polish-Lithuanian Commonwealth in the Eighteenth Century* (1991).

Orest Subtelny, *Domination of Eastern Europe: Native Nobilities and Foreign Absolutism, 1500–1715* (1986). Has aroused much disagreement.

Russia

Ivo Banac and Paul Bushkovitch (eds.), *The Nobility in Russia and Eastern Europe* (1983).

Jerome Blum, *Lord and Peasant in Russia from the Ninth to the Nineteenth Centuries* (1961).

Robert O. Crummey, *Aristocrats and Servitors: The Boyar Elite in Russia, 1618–1689* (1983).

Paul Dukes, *Catherine the Great and the Russian Nobility* (1967).

T. Emmons, *The Russian Landed Gentry and the Peasant Emancipation of 1861* (1968).

Robert E. Jones, *The Emancipation of the Russian Nobility, 1762–1785* (1973).

Marc Raeff, *Origins of the Russian Intelligentsia: The Eighteenth Century Nobility* (1966).

Themes

Jeroen Duindam, *Vienna and Versailles: The Courts of Europe's Dynastic Rivals, 1550–1780* (2003).

Mark Girouard, *The Victorian Country House* (1971).

Mark Girouard, *Life in the English Country House* (1978). A best-seller, but not always convincing.

Mark Girouard, *Life in the French Country House* (2000).

Mark Girouard, *The Return to Camelot: Chivalry and the English Gentleman* (1981).

V. G. Kiernan, *The Duel in European History: Honour and the Reign of Aristocracy* (1988).

Peter Mandler, *The Fall and Rise of the Stately Home* (1997). Brilliant survey, full of sharp insights.

Hugh Trevor-Roper, *The Plunder of the Arts in the Seventeenth Century* (1970).

Amanda Vickery, *The Gentleman's Daughter: Womens' Lives in Georgian England* (1999). Challenges the view that elite women were marginalized.

Martin Wiener, *English Culture and the Decline of the Industrial Spirit, 1850–1980* (1981). A tract for Thatcher's times that has perhaps not outlasted her.

Aristocratic voices

Most of the Roman historians wrote with aristocratic prejudices, but Cicero's *Letters to Atticus* give a clear sense of what was at stake for the ruling orders in the republic's last century. All well-educated nobles in later centuries knew them. A vivid picture of chivalric values in action is the epic of *Tiran lo Blanc*, devoured as late as the 18th century by Catherine the Great. Castiglione's *The Courtier* is the most important, and still very readable, handbook of aristocratic conduct. An English equivalent is Sir Thomas Elyot's *The Boke called the Governor*. Noble life under Louis XIV is elegantly chronicled in Mme de Sévigné's *Letters*, while the world of his court is reported and commented upon in incomparable detail through the voluminous *Memoirs* of the Duke de Saint-Simon. Chesterfield's *Letters to His Son* prescribe how to be a gentleman in the 18th century, while Montesquieu's contemporaneous

Spirit of the Laws reflects on the whole of aristocratic history in elaborating new rationales for noble behaviour. The memoirs of Princess Dashkov record the life of the Russian elite, at home and abroad, under Catherine, and the first volume of Alexander Herzen's describes a noble upbringing in early 19th-century Russia. The literary skill of Chateaubriand makes the memoirs he sold for posthumous publication a memorable romantic description of changing noble fortunes over the revolutionary and Napoleonic upheavals. The sad dissolution of the Irish Ascendancy is movingly portrayed in David Thompson, *Woodbrook*. A trivial romp through what was left of noble ideals by the mid-20th century is Nancy Mitford (ed.), *Noblesse Oblige: An Enquiry into the Identifiable Characteristics of the English Aristocracy* (1956).

Aristocracy in fiction

Cervantes's *Don Quixote* is perhaps the best-known petty nobleman in literature, ridiculed and admired in equal measure. On the eve of the French Revolution, the heartlessness of nobles was unblinkingly depicted by Goethe in *The Sorrows of Young Werther*, Choderlos de Laclos in *Dangerous Liaisons*, or Beaumarchais's play *The Marriage of Figaro*. Classic and timeless portrayals of the everyday values of gentlefolk are the novels of Jane Austen, particularly *Persuasion* and *Mansfield Park*. The obsessional hunting of Anthony Trollope gave him much first-hand material for the pictures of the Victorian landed classes found throughout his vast output, but particularly in the Palliser novels. See also R. Gilmour, *The Idea of the Gentleman in the Victorian Novel* (1981). The boredom of Russian noble life in the same century is amply chronicled, whether in Turgenev's *A Nest of Gentlefolk*, Gogol's *Dead Souls*, or Goncharov's *Oblomov*. The equivalent for France are the elegiac novels of Marcel Proust. A somewhat fawning celebration of the exclusivism of English Catholic aristocrats in the 20th century was Evelyn Waugh's *Brideshead Revisited*, subsequently made into a sumptuous television series based on one of the greatest of country houses, Castle Howard. And one of the best-selling novels of that century was turned into a superb film by the aristocratic Marxist Luchino Visconti: Prince Giuseppe di Lampedusa's *The Leopard* is a marvellous portrait of a traditional Sicilian grandee confronted by the social and political challenges of the 19th century.

Index

Index

Aristocracy

THE FRENCH REVOLUTION
A Very Short Introduction

William Doyle

Beginning with a discussion of familiar images of the French Revolution, garnered from Dickens, Baroness Orczy, and Tolstoy, this short introduction leads the reader to the realization that we are still living with the legacy of the French Revolution. It destroyed age-old cultural, institutional, and social structures in France and beyond. William Doyle shows how the *ancien régime* became *ancien* as well as examining cases in which achievement failed to match ambition, exploring its consequences in the arenas of public affairs and responsible government, and ending with thoughts on why the revolution has been so controversial.

'A brilliant combination of narrative and analysis, this masterly essay provides the best introduction to its subject in any language.'

Tim Blanning, University of Cambridge

www.oup.co.uk/isbn/0-19-285396-1

HISTORY
A Very Short Introduction
John H. Arnold

History: A Very Short Introduction is a stimulating essay about how we understand the past. The book explores various questions provoked by our understanding of history, and examines how these questions have been answered in the past. Using examples of how historians work, the book shares the sense of excitement at discovering not only the past, but also ourselves.

'A stimulating and provocative introduction to one of collective humanity's most important quests – understanding the past and its relation to the present. A vivid mix of telling examples and clear cut analysis.'

David Lowenthal, University College London

'This is an extremely engaging book, lively, enthusiastic and highly readable, which presents some of the fundamental problems of historical writing in a lucid and accessible manner. As an invitation to the study of history it should be difficult to resist.'

Peter Burke, Emmanuel College, Cambridge

www.oup.co.uk/vsi/history

ROMAN BRITAIN
A Very Short Introduction
Peter Salway

Britain was within the orbit of Graeco-Roman civilization for at least half a millenium, and for over 350 years part of the political union created by the Roman Empire that encompassed most of Europe and all the countries of the Mediterranean.

First published as part of the best-selling *Oxford Illustrated History of Britain*, Peter Salway's Very Short Introduction to Roman Britain weaves together the results of archaeological investigation and historical scholarship in a rounded and highly readable concise account. He charts the history of Britain from the first invasion under Julius Casear ro the final collapse of the Romano-British way of life in the 5th century AD.

www.oup.co.uk/isbn/0-19-285404-6

POLITICS
A Very Short Introduction
Kenneth Minogue

In this provocative but balanced essay, Kenneth Minogue discusses the development of politics from the ancient world to the twentieth century. He prompts us to consider why political systems evolve, how politics offers both power and order in our society, whether democracy is always a good thing, and what future politics may have in the twenty-first century.

'This is a fascinating book which sketches, in a very short space, one view of the nature of politics … the reader is challenged, provoked and stimulated by Minogue's trenchant views.'

Ian Davies, *Talking Politics*

'a dazzling but unpretentious display of great scholarship and humane reflection'

Neil O'Sullivan, University of Hull

NINETEENTH-CENTURY BRITAIN

A Very Short Introduction

Christopher Harvie & H. C. G. Matthew

First published as part of the best-selling Oxford Illustrated History of Britain, Christopher Harvie and H. C. G. Matthew's Very Short Introduction to nineteenth-century Britain is a sharp but subtle account of remarkable economic and social change – and an even more remarkable political stability. Britain in 1789 was overwhelmingly rural, agrarian, multilingual, and almost half Celtic. By 1914, when it faced its greatest test since the defeat of Napoleon, it was largely urban and English. Christopher Harvie and H. C. G. Matthew show the forces behind Britain's rise to its imperial zenith, and the continuing tensions within the nations and classes of the 'union state'.

www.oup.co.uk/isbn/0-19-285398-8

EIGHTEENTH-CENTURY BRITAIN

A Very Short Introduction

Paul Langford

Eighteenth-century Britain is sometimes thought of as sedate, oligarchical, and conservative. First published as part of the best-selling *Oxford Illustrated History of Britain*, Paul Langford's Very Short Introduction to eighteenth-century Britain reveals the essential vitality as Britain evolved into a great power, an industrial giant, and a dynamic commercial society. The transforming effect of a hundred years is concisely narrated in its diversity and complexity.

www.oup.co.uk/isbn/0-19-285399-6

THE SPANISH CIVIL WAR
A Very Short Introduction
Helen Graham

This Very Short Introduction offers a powerfully-written explanation of the war's complex origins and course, and explores its impact on a personal and international scale. It also provides an ethical reflection on the war in the context of Europe's tumultuous twentieth century, highlighting why it has inspired some of the greatest writers of our time, and how it continues to resonate today in Britain, continental Europe, and beyond.

This book examines Spanish participation in European resistance movements during World War II and also the ongoing civil war waged politically, economically, judicially and culturally inside Spain by Francoism after its military victory in 1939. It also indicates its ultimate failure in the return of Republican memory now occurring in Spain during the opening years of the twenty-first century.

> 'This is far and away the best short introduction to the Spanish Civil War that I have read in any language.'
> **Professor Paul Preston, European Institute, London School of Economics**

http://www.oup.co.uk/isbn/0–19–280377–8